RIP VAN WINKLE GOES TO THE PLAY

AND OTHER

ESSAYS ON PLAYS AND PLAYERS

RIP VAN WINKLE GOES TO THE PLAY

AND OTHER
ESSAYS ON PLAYS AND PLAYERS

BY

BRANDER MATTHEWS

EMERITUS PROFESSOR OF DRAMATIC LITERATURE IN COLUMBIA UNIVERSITY
MEMBER OF THE AMERICAN ACADEMY OF ARTS AND LETTERS

KENNIKAT PRESS, INC./PORT WASHINGTON, N. Y.

To

CLAYTON HAMILTON
AND
HATCHER HUGHES

YOUNG FRIENDS OF MY OLD AGE

CONTENTS

PAGE

I *Rip Van Winkle Goes to the Play* . . 1

II *Uncle Sam Exporter of Plays* . . . 25

III *What Is a "Well-Made" Play?* . . 47

IV *The Question of the Soliloquy* . . . 67

V *On the Right of an Author to Repeat Himself* 81

VI *Second-Hand Situations* 101

VII *Claptrap* 123

VIII *The Scene Is Laid* 141

IX *The Development of Scenic Devices* . 159

X *Memories of Actresses* 177

XI *The Art of Acting* 205

I

RIP VAN WINKLE GOES TO THE PLAY

I

RIP VAN WINKLE GOES TO THE PLAY

I

I HAVE been a playgoer from my youth up. At the early age of eight my mother's father, who was a Scot, took me to Laura Keene's to see 'Jeanie Deans,' Boucicault's dramatization of the 'Heart of Midlothian'; and I can still recall my thrilling suspense when the mob battered in the doors of the Tolbooth and swarmed over the stage. This was in the first month of 1860; and my Scotch grandfather had wanted me to see 'Jeanie Deans' because it was a Scotch play. Three years later, when I was scant eleven, I went with him to Niblo's Garden, where Edwin Forrest was appearing in 'Macbeth,' which was also a Scotch play.

In the next half-dozen years I gazed with joyous delight at the Ravels, those expert pantomimists; and I think that this delight was renewed more than once, as I remember the dying agonies of the almost human hero of 'Jocko, the Brazilian Ape,' and also a more mystifying spectacle in which a man had his arms and his legs cut off one by one and then

3

his head,—only to become whole again and indisputably alive after his severed members had been laid out on a magic table.

> Eheu fugaces, Posthume,
> How the years glide away and are lost to me!

Before I had attained to the more mature age of fourteen I beheld the 'Rosedale' of Lester Wallack, that native of New York who persisted in being an Englishman; and I can tremble again in dreadful anticipation when I revisualize the nocturnal visit of the ultra-heroic hero into the camp of the sleeping gipsies, to sing the old song which lured forth the stolen child of the hero's lady-love. A little before I had been fascinated by this heroic adventure, or a little later, I had the privilege of admiring Edwin Booth in 'Hamlet.' This was at the Winter Garden, where Shakspere's masterpiece was achieving its first run of one hundred consecutive performances. That was in 1864; and in the same year or the next I sat spellbound when Richelieu threatened to launch the Curse of Rome. The long and narrow playbill informed me that the scenery of both these plays, 'Hamlet' and 'Richelieu,' had been painted in Paris, an expensive novelty in those distant days when the wandering tragedian was expected to make the best of the stock scenery of the local theater, shabby as it

4

might be, and shopworn, and only infrequently appropriate.

In the summer of 1866 we went to Europe, to London—where I was captivated by an ethereal ballet at the Alhambra, and to Paris, where I paid my first visit to the Théâtre Français, which I was to know intimately ten and twenty years later. At this first visit to that venerable temple of the drama—venerable always yet endowed with the gift of eternal youth —the program included Musset's 'Il ne faut pas badiner avec l'amour'; and after nearly sixty years I can still hear Favart's despairing cry as she bade farewell to Delaunay—"Adieu, Perdican! Elle est morte!" A few months later came the Exposition of 1867; and we went to two comedy-dramas of the triumphantly successful Sardou, then in the first flush of his long continued productivity and popularity. Much as I was pleased by the dramaturgic dexterity and the journalistic wit of the 'Famille Benoiton' and of 'Nos Bons Villageois'—a dexterity and a wit that I was too young to appreciate but not too young to relish—I think that I found a more obvious pleasure in two superb spectacles, 'Cendrillon' at the Châtelet and the 'Biche aux Bois' at the Porte Saint Martin. Not until long after I had been charmed by the dazzling splendors of the 'Biche aux Bois' did I discover

5

that the prominent but unimportant part of the Princess had been played by a slim young woman who was in time to achieve world-wide notoriety as Sarah-Bernhardt.

We returned to New York late in the fall of 1867 in time for me to see the 'Black Crook,' then nearing the end of its prolonged run, and to attend the opening performance of its even more glittering successor, the 'White Fawn,' a performance that did not end until two o'clock in the morning. In the next five years when I was advancing from sixteen to twenty-one, I became an assiduous first-nighter, a less arduous calling half-a-century ago when there were only half-a-dozen theaters in New York than it is now when there are more than half-a-hundred. I was present at the opening and again at the closing of John Brougham's brief season at the theater behind the Fifth Avenue Hotel, soon to be managed by Augustin Daly. In the spring of 1869, I attended the opening of Edwin Booth's Theater when the manager appeared as *Romeo* and his young wife as *Juliet*, with Edwin Adams as *Mercutio* and Mark Smith as *Friar Lawrence;* and in the fall of 1909, almost exactly forty years later, I attended the opening of the New Theater, an enterprise even more ambitious than Booth's and not more fortunate.

In the twoscore years between 1869 and 1909

6

I saw every play and every player that deserved to be seen—and not a few that did not. A procession of actors of outstanding stature passed before my eyes, Forrest, Booth, Barrett, Jefferson, Florence, Davenport, Henry Irving; Charlotte Cushman, Clara Morris, Rose Eytinge and Ellen Terry; Ristori, Salvini and Rossi; Barnay and Seebach, Janauschek and Modjeska; Fechter and Coquelin, Sarah-Bernhardt and Réjane. And even longer is the bede-roll of the dramatists whose plays attracted me in the course of the revolving years—Boucicault and Robertson, Pinero and Henry Arthur Jones, Bronson Howard and Clyde Fitch, Gillette and Thomas, Sardou, Dumas and Dennery, Sudermann and Ibsen. These playwrights and these players march again through my memory, glorious as an army with banners.

Then, as it happened, fifteen or twenty years ago, my visits to the theater became less frequent; and in the past five or ten years they have been but few. It may be that my ardor had relaxed a little, although I doubt it. Circumstances made it difficult for me to go to the play even when I desired it. As the result of this enforced abstinence I have not been a diligent witness of the change which has taken place in the American theater in the opening decades of this century. My information about this

7

change has been necessarily more or less second-hand. I lack the sharp impression of the thing seen with my own eyes. I found myself, so far as the drama was concerned, living rather in the past than in the present.

Fate willed it that early in 1924 the restrictions upon my theatergoing were removed, when I had slowly recovered from a long illness, and when my physician advised me to mix with my fellow man as often as my strength would permit; he even went so far as to prescribe playgoing—a prescription which coincided with my inclination. So it was that after his long sleep Rip Van Winkle was able to awake and to see for himself the result of the things which had happened while he had been slumbering.

II

IT is not the incorrigible garrulity of a septuagenarian which has prompted me to this autobiographic prelude; rather is it that I want the readers of this chapter to perceive the peculiar experience I have had in the past few months. I cannot but think that there are aspects of our theater at the end of this first quarter of the twentieth century that I may be able to analyze more clearly than those can whose eyes have not been sealed in sleep for almost a score of years.

Even if I am wrong in thus thinking, I have at least the advantage of that longer perspective of playgoing which is the inexpugnable possession of the veteran lagging superfluous. So I propose to set down before they fade the impressions made on me in the past half-year by the American plays I have been privileged to enjoy, by the actors in those pieces, and by the methods of the producers who were responsible for the performance of them. I had best begin this report of a returned traveller by asserting boldly that these plays, these players and these methods are far more satisfactory than such things were when I was serving my apprenticeship as a student of the stage, long, long ago.

Until the last two decades of the nineteenth century there were few comedies or dramas of American authorship which were not feeble in their workmanship and false in their portrayal of life. Before those two decades we were content to import our plays across the ocean from the English, who were then importing their plays across the Channel from the French. We had to feed on the London perversions of Parisian pieces, a fare as indigestible as it was innutritious. Nor was our table much better supplied when we began to import directly from France and Germany and to do our own perverting. Olive Logan turned the delicious 'Niniche' into

9

an unappetizing 'Newport'; and Daly played havoc with a host of German comedy-farces, disguising their foreign flavor with tasteless American sauce. I cannot declare too vehemently my belief that an adaptation whereby an alien story is maltreated in a vain effort to make it conform to our native manners and customs is the abomination of desolation.

On the other hand, a conscientious translation of an exotic masterpiece may be a thing of beauty and a joy forever. Such is Brian Hooker's consummately skilful rendering of Rostand's 'Cyrano de Bergerac'; such also is the workmanlike translation of Ibsen's 'Ghosts' made by William Archer. As New York is the most cosmopolitan of cities, and also the most hospitable to visitors from overseas, it is fit and proper that the most interesting plays of every alien tongue should be presented to our playgoers in their integrity, with only such condensation as our clearer skies and more bracing winds may make advisable. It is a good omen that while translations are not now infrequent, adaptations are rapidly losing favor. The finer the foreign play, the less likely it now is to be insulted by inartistic transmogrification. This is a great gain, not only because it increases our more exact understanding of what is being done by the playwrights of continental Europe, French and German, Italian and Spanish, Russian and Hungarian, but more especially because it provides us with helpful models for the sincere treatment of our own life.

In his illuminating study of the epochs of French drama, Brunetière asserted that "every nation is most easily interested in subjects from its own life present or past, or from those of kindred races." An exotic theme has always to wait for a tardy welcome, whereas every attempt to mirror our own characteristics is likely to be more immediately profitable. Half-a-century ago there were attempts to mirror American life which were profitable altho not estimable. 'Solon Shingle,' the 'Gilded Age,' the 'Mighty Dollar' were poor things even if they were our own, artificial, arbitrary, amorphous and empty, with no roots in reality and with no tincture of literature. A play of this kind was acceptable to our playgoers because it contained highly colored caricatures of American character; and it was acceptable for the moment only, in default of any more veracious rendering of the superficial aspects of American manners. Even Bronson Howard's brisk and bustling 'Saratoga' (produced as late as 1870) was so lacking in observation that it represented its imperfectly monogamous hero as receiving half-a-dozen challenges to a duel.

Bronson Howard was a dramatist of indisputable endowment. He was a born playwright; he had a firm hold on the unchanging principles of dramatic art; he had a piercing insight into the conditions of American life; but, alas! he was born out of time and he was subdued to what he worked in. As I have suggested elsewhere, if he had arrived twenty or thirty years later, when he could have put forth his full power, he might have been a leader in the present revival of the drama in English literature.

In the final weeks of the theatrical season of 1923-4 I saw a dozen plays of native authorship; one of them had its scene laid in a foreign land and another was based upon a foreign original; ten of them dealt with American life and character. I may as well list the titles of these ten plays before I comment on them; they were 'Hell-bent for Heaven,' the 'Merry Wives of Gotham,' the 'Show Off,' 'In the Next Room,' 'Helena's Boys,' 'Expressing Willie,' the 'Goose Hangs High,' 'Meet the Wife,' the 'Potters' and 'Rain.' They were all more or less successful; and each of them deserved such success as it attained. I do not wish to imply that they were all of them masterpieces of dramatic art, or even minor masterpieces; but in their several degrees they gave me the special pleasure that I

seek in the theater. Nor do I desire to suggest
that they were of equal merit, for of course they
varied widely in value. Some were slight and
superficial; but all were clever; and no one was
flagrantly false to the facts of life, even if more
than one was unable wholly to conceal its artifices. Taken by and large, they displayed a
freshness of topic, a fertility of invention, an
ingenuity of plotting, a neatness of construction
and an adroitness of craftsmanship, which would
have been sought in vain in even the best of the
native plays of half-a-century ago.

Two of them, 'Rain' and 'Hell-bent for
Heaven,' were veracious interpretations of human nature, inspired by imagination, inviting
and rewarding comparison with the work of the
most dexterous living dramatists of Europe.
These two plays, and some of the others also,
are good auguries for the future of the American
drama. I have reasons of my own for liking
'Hell-bent for Heaven,' but these reasons do not
inhibit me from expressing my high respect for
'Rain.' Both dramas deal with religious fanat-
icism and both enlarge our understanding of our
fellow man and of our fellow American; and to
say this is to say that they deserve well of those
who rejoice at the intensifying rivalry of the
play with the novel. After all, the ultimate
purpose of fiction, in the study or on the stage,

is to hold the mirror up to nature and to people our memories with human beings who are worth remembering and whom we cannot forget.

There is no need to dissect in detail these two plays or the other eight; but attention may be called to one quality they have in common: they are all of them well written, in clear and clean English, vigorous and unpretentious, uncontaminated by "fine writing" falsely so called. Without parading it they possess "literary merit"; and I make bold to believe that several of them will prove to be permanent additions to American literature, as readable as they are actable. Some of them are serious in theme, and in these the dialog has the stark directness of tense emotion; but no one of them is solemn, since their loftiest moments are accentuated by humorous touches, as is the case in real life, where tragedy and comedy are inextricably intertwined. They all eschew the old-fashioned and outworn "comic relief" which forced the funny characters to succeed the graver, whereby we were presented first with a streak of fat and then with a streak of lean. Making a more artistic use of the comic spirit they introduce us to men and women who are not mere figures of fun, but recognizable human beings, occasionally laughable because they are always human. Sometimes they attain to the higher levels of true comedy, which compels us to think even while we laugh.

For the most part their humor is good humor, not pitiless but consoling; and their wit is pleasantly mirthful, not acid or acrid. Their dialog is easy and seemingly natural, often felicitous with an unexpected turn of phrase. Moreover the talk whereby the action is carried on is not bespattered with verbal spangles, with what are loosely termed "epigrams," cynical sayings clipped from a note-book and wilfully pinned into the dialog. The characters speak for themselves, and out of their own hearts; they are not mere megaphones through which the author promulgates his own ideas, insistent on our attention to the moral or the thesis he believes himself to be inculcating.

III

AFTER saying my say thus succinctly about ten American plays which I have recently enjoyed I am glad to be able to praise with as little qualification the players who made these dramas and these comedies start to life on the stage. Taken together these dramas and these comedies were more adequately and more delicately acted than they would have been by the actors of my youth. The praisers of past times (whom we always have with us) look longingly back to what they call the "palmy days" of acting; they assert that we have now no performers of dominating personality with the consummate skill and the commanding authority of Charlotte Cushman, Edwin Booth, and Joseph Jefferson. They declare vehemently that altho we may have twenty separate dollars we have not now a single double eagle,—overlooking the fact that we need silver every day, whereas gold is necessary only on rarer occasions. It is a fact,—I can testify to it—that in the palmy days we were likely to have the double eagle, accompanied by a handful of pennies, with the inevitable result that the gold coin suffered from its contact with the copper pieces. Macready's diary is an unceasing wail over the careless incompetence of the actors who supported him; and when Edwin Booth opened his own spacious and splendid theater in 1869 there were not lacking shrill animadversions on the inferiority of the company he had himself engaged.

One reason for the difference of opinion between the praisers of the past and the praisers of the present lies in the divergence of their point of view, of their standards, of their ideals. This is due to the many changes in the physical conditions of performance. In the days of Macready and of Booth the theater had an "apron," thrust far out into the auditorium; and on this projecting platform, surrounded on three sides by the audience, the robust and full-lunged performer spouted the magniloquent speeches of an ultra-rhetorical drama—speeches "that you could sink your teeth in." In our day, the apron has been cut back; the curtain rises and falls in the proscenium arch, that has thereby become a picture frame behind which the actors of our time—constantly cautioned not "to get out of the picture"—speak the straightforward words of our unrhetorical plays. This alteration of the playhouse has forced a corresponding modification of the methods of the player. Our actors may have lost some-thing of the largeness of style demanded by the older type of play, but they have made up for this by their conquest of simplicity of utterance and by their subtler refinements in characteriza-tion. They are not in close contact with the spectators; and they are no longer called upon to deliver confidential asides to the audience. They do not now "take the stage," striding across it triumphantly, after a bravura speech; they are less likely to act each for himself and sometimes at the expense of the others present at the time; they have learned the value of team-play; and the result is a more harmonious whole.

In the stock companies of sixty years ago
every performer was rigidly restricted to his
own "line of business"—leading man and leading woman, old man and old woman, low comedian and light comedian, heavy man and
singing chambermaid. Therefore the parts they
impersonated were types rather than characters;
they were parts cut according to traditional pat-
terns, painted in the primary colors, so that the
spectators could recognize at once what manner
of man or woman each of the actors was supposed to represent. This practice may have
made for boldness and breadth; and perhaps it
was more or less necessary when plays were
pitchforked on the stage in slapdash fashion
with scant rehearsal and even scanter direction,
and when an actor might appear in three pieces
in a single evening and in a dozen in a single
week. Moreover, if there was a part in an important play which was not within the compass
of any actor in the company, it had none the
less to be undertaken by somebody, however
unfitted he might be. Special engagements
were infrequent and rarely possible; and the
manager had to make out as best he could with
the material he had. As a result there were
likely to be always one or two round pegs in
square holes.

To-day the author and the manager can call

to their assistance a "producer" who is the successor of the happy-go-lucky "stage-manager," and who is more competent than his predecessor and more powerful in his control of the performance. The producer studies the manuscript; he advises with the author; and he decides upon both the strategy and the tactics required to make explicit all that is implicit in the manuscript. He recommends the several actors and actresses who can best be trusted to impersonate the several parts, that is to say, who will look and speak as the characters ought to look and speak, and who will be able to rise to the full height of the situations in which these characters reveal themselves. This is called "casting to type"; and, altho it is sometimes carried to unhappy extremes, it results more often than not in a far more satisfactory rendering of the important figures of the play than was possible in the stock companies of yore with the cast-iron law of "lines of business" and with leading men and leading women who were not seldom far too advanced in years to be acceptable as youthful heroes and heroines.

The producer is also responsible for the scenery which is prepared especially for every new play, and which is less flamboyant than the stage-settings of threescore years ago; it is intended to be unobtrusive and to suggest (rather than to supply) an appropriate background for the action. Furthermore, the producer has now at his service a heterogeny of devices which enable him to achieve a discriminating delicacy in the lighting of the stage, an illumination which can be modified with a subtlety unsuspected by the spectators but none the less potent in evoking their emotional response as the story unrolls itself.

The producer has a function similar to that of the conductor of a symphony orchestra. He sets the tempo of the performance and he modifies this at will, accelerating the movement at one moment and retarding it at another, alternating his fortissimo and his pianissimo, stimulating the sluggishness of the laggards and curbing the excessive zeal of the more venturesome and individualistic, and finally (if he is a master of his art) attaining a unity of effect, a harmony of tone, a proportion and a symmetry, which force us to forget that we are seeing acting and bestow on us the illusion that what we are beholding is not fiction but fact. The producer, like the orchestral conductor, is a member of a new profession; and it is he who with his skill, his sympathy, his observation and his imagination, makes possible performances as perfect as those of 'Rain' and 'Hell-bent for Heaven'—a perfection which was not only impossible but almost inconceivable in the palmy days of old. We are profiting now by the development of the art of the producer, an art evolved from that of the earlier stage-manager —just as the skyscraper has been evolved from the log cabin. To him we owe the smoothness, the certainty, the apparent inevitability, of the performances of the ten American plays which I have listed. The plays were good in themselves, each after its kind; and the performances were worthy of them.

IV

OF course, our modern method, like everything else in this transitory world, has the defects of its qualities. The actor does not now find it as easy to acquire versatility; he is likely to be confined to parts of a similar type; and he may be called upon to appear in the same character in the same play for several hundred nights, whereby his work tends to become monotonous and unprofitable. Furthermore he has fewer opportunities of appearing in the classics, in the plays of Shakspere and of Sheridan and of thereby acquiring the breadth and the authority which come from the assumption of characters less realistic than those of our contemporary drama. I confess to having had a fear that the

delivery of blank verse might become one of the
lost arts, and that even the robust prose of the
older comedies might be beyond the scope of
actors who have had few or no opportunities to
essay themselves in stalwart and richly colored
characters. But I have taken heart of hope,
since the altogether admirable revival of 'Cyrano
de Bergerac' has shown me that the secret of
blank verse can be imparted to inexperienced
actors, and since the revival of 'She Stoops to
Conquer' made it plain that performers accustomed to the plays which require them not to
get out of the picture were able to acquit themselves nobly in plays where there was no picture
to get out of.

There is yet another unavoidable disadvantage of the system of "casting to type" in a
company engaged only for the "run of the play."
Meritorious pieces can no longer be kept in
stock, so to speak, ready for revival at a week's
notice. When the special company is once
scattered, there is little chance of getting it together again; and a revival of the piece in which
it appeared has to be a special production, almost as onerous and as risky as its original performance. As Señor Ibañez has put it sharply,
"a sort of tunnel, a tunnel of forgetfulness, as
it were, opens at the end of every dramatic run;
and into this tunnel all plays, however brilliant

their careers, ultimately make their way; and only the masterpiece, the exceptional production, succeeds in reappearing at the other end—years, and perhaps generations afterward." This is as undeniable as it is unfortunate; and as I call the roll of the ten American plays I have seen in swift succession, I find myself wondering whether I shall ever be able to see them again. Perhaps there are only two in the list, 'Rain' and 'Hell-bent for Heaven,' which the next generation of playgoers will have the privilege of enjoying in the theater, the only place where a play can disclose its full power.

And yet, when all is said, I am convinced that the methods of to-day are better than those of yesterday, and that (since we cannot have everything) we have good reason to be content with what we have.

(1924)

II

UNCLE SAM EXPORTER OF PLAYS

II

UNCLE SAM EXPORTER OF PLAYS

I

WHEN the erudite historian of French Literature, Gustave Lanson, spent a winter
in New York as exchange professor at Columbia
University, in the first decade of this century,
he chanced to read a high-school text-book on
American literature; and when he next met the
writer of this primer he said smilingly: "What
seemed to me most significant in your book was
a chapter I did not find in it—a chapter on the
American drama." As it happened, the author
of the schoolbook was a professor of dramatic
literature; and he found himself regretfully explaining that he had not dealt with the drama,
because there had been composed in the United
States in the nineteenth century few plays important enough to demand critical consideration. No one of the conspicuous figures in
American literature had been a playwright.
There were poets and story-tellers, essayists and
historians and orators; but there had been no
outstanding dramatist. And even in the comprehensive four-volume Cambridge 'History of

American Literature' there are only two chapters on the drama; and the writers of these two chapters had to make their bricks with a scant supply of straw.

It was not until we come toward the end of the nineteenth century and until we find Bronson Howard companioned by Clyde Fitch, William Gillette and Augustus Thomas that the successful plays of native authorship were sufficiently solid in material and in structure to deserve careful criticism. In the mid-years of the last century there were popular pieces, sometimes very popular indeed, which presented lively American characters, many of them so highly colored as to be on the verge of caricature and most of them framed in plots of flimsy artificiality, now sinking into the triviality of farce and then stiffening into the arbitrariness of melodrama. They may have had, and in fact not a few of them did have, a superficial veracity, but they had no roots in assured observation of American life and American conditions. 'Mose' and 'Kit,' 'Solon Shingle,' the 'Gilded Age' and the 'Mighty Dollar' are not known even by name except to specialists in theatrical history. Only 'Rip Van Winkle,' as embodied by Jefferson, survives in the memory of elderly playgoers. There was truth in the sharp saying attributed to Dion Boucicault in the eighth decade of the nineteenth century: "All the Americans seem to recognize as dramatic is the caricature of character; and that is what the successful plays are—caricature of eccentric character set in a weak dramatic framework."

There is this to be said, however, that feeble as these pieces were in plotting and empty as they were of substance, they represented a movement in the right direction. They did attempt, however imperfectly, to deal with our own life and to set before us our own fellow citizens. They were pitifully inadequate, no doubt, and yet they had this one quality, that they were not colonial imitations of life as it was lived in some other country, in England, for instance. More than forty years ago I pointed out that if, as De Quincey says, "the acknowledged duty of comedy" is to "fathom the coynesses of human nature and to arrest the fleeting phenomena of human demeanor," then the writers of these crude pieces were wofully remiss, since they had neither fathomed coynesses nor arrested phenomena. And in those now distant days, I also quoted another remark of De Quincey's that "Comedy, as the reflex of the current social life, will shift in correspondence to the shifting movements of civilization" and that therefore "inevitably as human intercourse in cities grows more refined, comedy will grow

29

more subtle; it will build itself on distinctions of character less grossly defined, and on features of manners more delicate and impalpable." If De Quincey was right, the shifting movement of our civilization is to be credited with a share in the comparative refinement of our more recent comedy and with its more delicate discrimination of character.

It must needs be noted also that not only in the United States was there a penury of playwrights able to fathom the coynesses of human nature and to depict the impalpable features of manners; there was in the same period from 1825 to 1875 a poverty almost as pitiable in Great Britain and in Germany, in Italy and in Spain. In the mid-years of the nineteenth century the drama was alive and vigorously vital only in France. And oddly enough the productivity of the French playwrights—their ingenuity, their inventiveness, was largely responsible for the dearth of indigenous drama in the other countries of Europe, because (as there was then no satisfactory international stage right), the managers of theaters in the United States, in England and Germany, in Spain and in Italy, could help themselves without payment to the plays which had pleased the fastidious playgoers of Paris. So it was that the native playwrights of other lands had to vend their wares in an unfair competition with stolen goods.

In Great Britain a large majority of the plays produced in the mid-years of the nineteenth century were translations or adaptations from the French; and in the United States the situation was even sadder, since the few American playwrights had as rivals the British adapters as well as the French authors of the original plays. And worse remains behind, for that was an epoch of great actors and actresses, who naturally preferred to perform the great characters created by Shakspere, and also the less vigorous but still effective parts devised by the nineteenth-century imitators of Shakspere, Sheil, Banim, and Sheridan Knowles. Whenever we have acquainted ourselves with all the adverse circumstances of the American theater, we find ourselves wondering not at the sparsity of American dramatists but at the existence of the few who were able to accomplish even the little they did manage to achieve.

II

If this was the unhappy situation in the middle of the nineteenth century, the situation at the beginning of that century was still more unfortunate. Most of the actors and actresses

in American theaters a hundred years ago were
British by birth; and naturally enough they
were prone to regard with contempt the sporadic
efforts at dramatic authorship ventured upon
by aspiring American writers. They did not
believe that anything worthy of their acting
could be produced by a native of the United
States; and when we recall even the best of
these American attempts, we must admit that
they had not a little justification for their hos-
tile attitude. Moreover, as many of them had
come from London, they found it hard to accept the conditions of a community which still
revealed many evidences of its frontier strug-
gling. Some of these actors, no doubt, longed
to return to the right little, tight little island
and had small affection for the land of their
adoption. A few of them may have been in the
state of mind of a more recent visitor, a British
actor who (so Mr. George Arliss has told us)
happened to stumble as he was descending the
gang-plank of the steamer which had brought
him over, and who, as he picked himself up,
was heard to ejaculate, "I knew I shouldn't
like this blasted country!"

In the 'Personal Recollections of the Stage'
of William B. Wood, long the manager of the
leading theater in Philadelphia, there is an
anecdote which demands quotation here. At

Wood's request Scott's 'Marmion' had been dramatized by James N. Barker, a fellow Philadelphian; and it was produced in 1813, that is to say, in the middle of the War of 1812. Wood tells us that several earlier pieces of Barker's had failed solely because they were known to be the work of an American. Wood was confident that the dramatization of 'Marmion' would prove attractive, if only he could conceal from both the British actors and the American audiences the fact that it was the work of an American playwright:

I knew the then prejudice against any native play and concocted with Cooper a very innocent fraud upon the public. We insinuated that the piece was a London one, had it sent to our theater from New York, where it was made to arrive in the midst of a rehearsal, in the presence of the actors, packed up exactly like pieces we were in the habit of receiving from London. It was opened with great gravity, and announced without any author being alluded to. None of the company were in the secret, as I well knew these actors cannot keep counsel, not even the prompter. It was played with great success for six or seven nights, when, believing it safe, I announced the author, and from that moment it *ceased to attract*. This is not a very creditable story but a true one.

Wood added that Cooper produced the same play in New York a little later, "without a hint as to its author"; and here Wood's memory was at fault, for Cooper in New York went further in deception than Wood had done in Philadelphia; he announced 'Marmion' as by Thomas Morton (a British playwright once well known as the author of 'Speed the Plough'). And a recent examination of Wood's own book of nightly receipts has shown that there was, in fact, no great falling off after Barker's authorship was acknowledged.

This was in 1813; and in the following half-century the proportion of native actors kept on increasing. Quite possibly also the prejudice of the imported performers against plays of domestic manufacture sensibly diminished. Yet it is only a little more than fifty years ago that Lester Wallack, who was British to the backbone (altho he had been born in New York), could not make up his mind to produce 'Drum-Taps,' a Civil War play of Bronson Howard's. This alien manager of the leading New York theater might be willing to overlook the American authorship but he would not accept the American theme. "Couldn't you make it the Crimea?" he asked plaintively. It is to Howard's honor that he refused this suggestion, altho it must have had its allurement for an ambitious and untried playwright; and it was to Howard's profit also since he was able so to

34

improve this 'prentice work that under the title of 'Shenandoah' it had a memorable success.

It may be that Lester Wallack knew what his public wanted; it was accustomed to expect in his theater the pick of the plays which had been profitable in London. Perhaps even in 1870 the playgoers of the chief city of the United States had no great confidence in the aspiring playwrights of their own country. I recall having seen in a comic paper of those distant days a sketch, representing a dramatic critic finishing his dinner and ordering his cup of coffee: "And please make it strong. I'm going to see an American comedy this evening, and I must keep awake if I can!"

If we may judge by the rhymed prolog which Epes Sargent wrote for Anna Cora Mowatt's 'Fashion' when that comedy was produced in 1845, the American public was then devoid of any predilection for American plays:

"Fashion, A comedy." I'll go—but stay,
Now I read further, 'tis a native play!
Bah! Home-made calicoes are well enough,
But home-made dramas must be stupid stuff.
Had it the London stamp 'twould do—but then
For plays we lack the manners and the men.

35

III

ONCE more we have to confess that most of our home-made dramas were stupid stuff. But there was one native American playwright who won a modest reputation in England more than a century ago, John Howard Payne. His position, however, is peculiar. He was an American who went to England and resided there and made adaptations of French pieces for the British managers. His plays were scarcely ever original; they were not written in the United States and then exported to Great Britain; they were prepared for the London market on the spot. None the less is it to be recorded that Payne was the first American dramatist to have a play performed in Paris. He compiled a tragedy for Edmund Kean, borrowing freely from the many predecessors who had dealt with the same historic character; and when the English tragedian went over to Paris in 1828 to act with an English company, he appeared at least once in Payne's 'Brutus or the Fall of Tarquin.'

There were other native American playwrights whose pieces withstood the voyage across "the salt, unplumbed estranging sea" in the years when Payne was finding it hard

36

to earn his living as a theatrical hack in England. Geneste, the historian of the London stage, records that the 'Pocahontas' of James N. Barker (the dramatizer of 'Marmion') was acted at Drury Lane in 1820. This seems to have been done without the privity of the author, who had published his play. Apparently the piece did not prove attractive to the British playgoers; yet it is noteworthy as being the earliest play on an American theme by an American writer to be produced outside the United States.

In the next half-century there were sporadic appearances of American plays in London, for the most part, the result of the transatlantic tours of American stars, male and female. We began early to export actors to England in a vain effort to recover the balance of trade. The first of these voyagers was Thomas Apthorpe Cooper, who was British by birth but who was accepted in England as American—just as Ada Rehan and Julia Marlowe were later to be acclaimed there as Americans. Cooper was followed by Hackett and by J. S. Silsbee, by Edwin Forrest and Charlotte Cushman, by Anna Cora Mowatt, Edwin Booth and Lawrence Barrett. Professor A. H. Quinn (the historian of the American drama) has kindly supplied me with the titles of the American plays taken over the

37

ocean by one or another of these histrionic adventurers. Silsbee acted in the 'Forest Rose' of Samuel Woodworth (still remembered as the lyrist of the 'Old Oaken Bucket') for a hundred nights in London, a remarkable run a century ago. In London and in 1836 Forrest acted in the 'Gladiator' of Robert Montgomery Bird (still remembered as the writer of 'Nick of the Woods,' that best of dime novels). In 1850 Mrs. Mowatt acted in her own 'Armand, or the Child of the People,' the subtitle being altered to the 'Peer and the Peasant' in deference to British susceptibility.

To these performances by American actors who brought their plays with them, it is possible to add a few other performances of American pieces by British actors. 'Velasco' by Epes Sargent was produced at the Marylebone Theater in 1849 by E. L. Davenport. 'Calaynos' by George H. Boker was produced by Samuel Phelps at the Sadler's Wells Theater in 1849, without consultation with the author, who had parted with his control over the play by publishing it. And Boker's 'Betrothal' was played in London in 1853. This is a sorry showing for the first sixty years of the nineteenth century. The exporting of American plays remained infrequent and infelicitous; and all through this period American theaters were

38

devoted mainly to British plays and to British adaptations.

In fact, the earliest American playwright to establish himself in the favor of London audiences was Bronson Howard. His brisk and bustling five-act farce 'Saratoga,' produced in New York in 1869, was anglicized by Frank Marshall, condensed into three acts, renamed 'Brighton' and acted in London in 1874 by Charles Wyndham. A later farce, 'Hurricanes,' was first seen in New York in 1878, and as 'Truth' was performed by Wyndham in London in 1879. And Howard's 'Banker's Daughter' (New York, 1878) was anglicized by James Alberry (London, 1879), with an alteration of its name to the 'Old Love and the New.' There is a certain significance in the fact that these three American plays had to have their action transferred to England; at least it seems to show that the British playgoer was then less cosmopolitan than the American playgoer, who did not demand that an alien drama should be Americanized.

In more recent years William Gillette's 'Held by the Enemy' and 'Secret Service' were allowed to retain their American atmosphere. So were the 'Alabama,' 'Arizona' and 'Earl of Pawtucket' of Augustus Thomas. So were half-a-dozen of the plays of Clyde Fitch. Apparently the insularity of the British has diminished as their familiarity with the works of alien authors has increased; and most of the French plays which are now to be seen on the London stage are allowed to remain French and no longer compelled to disguise themselves as British. So far as I could learn from a distance of three thousand miles no one of the ten or a dozen plays of American authorship which were acted in London in 1920 was forced to suffer a sea change and to pretend to be what it was not. Quite possibly the British playgoer is acquiring a taste for the flavor of exotic drama, and is getting to like our plays because they are American and not in spite of it. But I have seen of late more than one insular protest against the "American invasion" of the English theaters. Thus does Time bring its revenges.

It is worthy of remark that the willingness of British audiences to be amused by pieces of American authorship became so obvious toward the end of the nineteenth century that the late Charles Frohman relaxed his energy as a producer of untried plays, to settle down as an importer and exporter of the drama. He found his profit in bringing to New York pieces which had been prosperous in London and in taking over to London pieces which had proved their attractiveness in New York. Thus it was at last that the trade-winds of the drama blew alternately from west to east, and from east to west, instead of blowing continuously from east to west, as they had been wont to do a century earlier.

IV

WHILE the playwrights of the United States were thus making themselves known to our kin across the sea, they found it far less easy to get a foothold on the continent where a community of speech and of literary tradition did not assist them. I have already noted that Payne's 'Brutus,' written for a British actor, was performed at least once in Paris nearly a century ago when an English-speaking company was appearing in the French capital; and I must now note that another American, Marion Crawford, wrote his 'Francesca da Rimini' in French for Mme. Sarah-Bernhardt, a tragedy which, oddly enough, has not yet been translated into English.

The Parisian playwrights had earlier levied on American novelists. Scribe had based one of his pieces on the 'Lionel Lincoln' of Fenimore Cooper; Ferdinand Dugué had dramatized 'Leatherstocking'; and Dennery had prepared an 'Uncle Tom's Cabin' of his own. Later Meilhac had utilized 'Rip Van Winkle' in the

41

libretto of a light opera. In time 'Bas de Cuir' and the 'Case de l'Oncle Tom' and 'Rip, Légende Americaine' were followed by 'Le Petit Lord,' a version of 'Little Lord Fauntleroy' and by 'La Belle de New York.' Not to be omitted are the French adaptations of 'Secret Service' and of 'Baby Mine.' And there are doubtless not a few other dramas of American origin which have been presented to Parisian playgoers in the opening years of this century.

With the stage in Germany and in Italy I am not so familiar as I am with that in France; and one or more of these French adaptations of American plays may have been found useful by German or Italian companies. The Germans and the Italians were in the habit of taking over French plays; and it would be easy for them to enlarge their repertories by including pieces originally written in English, whether British or American would matter little.

So far as I know the earliest American play to be performed in Berlin was a German version of the British alteration of Bronson Howard's 'Saratoga'; it was entitled 'Seine Erste und Einziger Liebe,' and its chief part was acted in German by Charles Wyndham. And one of the latest American plays to draw crowded houses in Berlin is 'Potash and Perlmutter.' In Italy the earliest American playwright to win favor

42

was Clyde Fitch. I recall his telling me that the finest performance of his 'Truth' that he had ever witnessed was in Rome. 'Truth,' I may remark, bid fair to achieve the cosmopolitan popularity of Ibsen's 'Doll's House,' of Sudermann's 'Magda' and of Pinero's 'Second Mrs. Tanqueray,' because, like these dissimilar social dramas, it contained a dominating character alluring to ambitious actresses of every nationality.

The reasons why American plays are now exported widely are not far to seek. In the first place there is to-day a substantial uniformity in the playhouses of the civilized world. The formulas of playmaking devised in Paris about the middle of the nineteenth century are to-day common property. A drama in English differs from a drama in Italian or in German only in its content, and not at all in its procedure. Therefore any modern play is portable, transportable, exportable, and importable. A Hungarian drama (however much its moral may be betrayed by translation) demands no modification of its method; it finds itself instantly at home in England and in Italy, in Scandinavia and in France; it may amuse alien audiences or it may annoy them; but they have not to adjust themselves to a different technic.

That is one reason; and another can be found

43

in a change of heart on the part of the French. They are no longer satisfied with the "well-made" play such as Scribe and Sardou were skilful in manufacturing, the piece which depended almost altogether on its purely theatrical effectiveness. They are now charging their dramas with a deeper meaning; their leading playwrights are probing more subtly into human nature; they are dealing more directly with life and character, with social conditions and with social problems. As a result their plays, more intellectual but perhaps less emotional, are firmly rooted in the soil of France itself. By this fact therefore they are less likely to be attractive to foreigners unfamiliar with French society. A piece with a plot, with a succession of boldly emotional situations, is as effective in one tongue as in another; it has an almost universal appeal. But a study of social conditions peculiar to France is likely to prove uninteresting to those who do not know these conditions. This is why the masterpiece of French comedy in the seventeenth century, the 'Misanthrope' of Molière, has never won a welcome outside of France; and the same fate has befallen the masterpieces of French comedy in the eighteenth century and in the nineteenth, the 'Mariage de Figaro' of Beaumarchais and the 'Gendre de M. Poirier' of Augier and Sandeau.

44

I make bold to believe that in the United States to-day at the close of this first quarter of this twentieth century there can be seen an ingenuity in plot-making, and a fertility in devising situations recalling that which was to be observed in France in the days of Scribe and Dennery and Sardou and in Spain in the days of Lope de Vega and Calderon, two periods of dramaturgic dexterity and of abundant productivity. The American faculty of invention, which has filled the world with Yankee contrivances, seems to have been directed suddenly to the construction of plays. I am aware that to say this is to lay myself open to the retort that our plays are as machine-made as our Yankee contrivances, and even that we are engaged in quantity-production rather than quality-production. If thus cornered I should have to confess that there may be more than a little truth in the charge; but I should proffer as my rejoinder the statement that not a few of the American plays of this century are as interesting in the library as they are in the theater. Then I should urge that just now we are perhaps too close to the forest to see the trees. Furthermore, I should point out that a luxuriant undergrowth may contain the potency of a tree or two of exceptional stature. And finally, as one who loves the theater for its own sake, I

45

should insist that a play effective on the stage is always welcome, even if it fails to win our affection in the study.

At least our stage is now independent of the foreign playwrights. The fact is—and facts are inexorable—that of the hundred farces and comedies and dramas of one kind or another which were produced in the playhouses of New York in the season of 1920–1, seventy had been written on this side of the Atlantic and only thirty-five had been provided for us by European dramatists. Fifty years ago I doubt if one-fifth of the pieces acted in New York were to be credited to native authors. To-day two-thirds are of our own manufacture. If we look on this picture and on this, we may well take heart of hope.

(1922)

III

WHAT IS A "WELL-MADE" PLAY?

III

WHAT IS A "WELL–MADE" PLAY?

I

I RISE to a personal explanation. At midnight on June 30, 1924, I ceased to be a professor of dramatic literature. I retired from active service into innocuous desuetude and was transferred to the Officers Reserve Corps. A fortnight later, this event, important to me, however unimportant to any one else, was commented upon by a critic for whose gracious words I here express my gratitude. Upon some of these words, however, I am moved to comment in my turn:

Professor Matthews, and his followers after him, liked the "well-made play"; and they, if not he, made it a fetish. Such a program was tempting, particularly so long as there was a contemporary dearth of plays which had any real literary merit. It fortified playwrights and critics in their instinct to see a necessity as a virtue. . . . When later a new age of drama dawned, the followers of Professor Matthews were some of them not ready for it. They kept on talking about Pinero when there was a Shaw to talk about.

Now, when I read that I asked myself what it was that the kindly commentator had in

mind when he used the term "well-made play,"
putting it in quotation-marks. If he used it,—
as I think he did—with a glance back at the
praise which Francisque Sarcey was wont to
give to a play with complicated machinery, dexterously adjusted to produce the utmost of theatrical effect, then I can only regret that any
follower of mine,—if such there be—should have
made that sort of thing into a fetish; and I desire to disclaim all responsibility for his, her or
their misdeeds. But if,—as I do not think he
did,—he meant to imply that there was a possibly superior kind of play which because of its
content did not need to be well made, then I
cannot but join issue with him, confessing my
ineradicable conviction that my followers (be
they few or many) are absolutely in the right
in making a fetish out of the art of construction.

To the best of my belief the term "well-made
play" (in quotation-marks, if you please) was
invented by Sarcey at the time when he was
protesting strenuously and unceasingly against
the laxity of construction, the disregard of the
essential principles of playmaking which he
found in many of the pieces produced by An-
toine at the Théâtre Libre, pieces which the
Naturalists gleefully hailed as "slices of life,"
that is to say, a series of successive episodes not
integrally related. Sarcey was a man of letters,

a scholar of parts, a graduate of the Ecole Nor-
male in the same class with Taine and About,
a devout interpreter of the French classics, Corneille and Racine, Molière and Beaumarchais.
Man of the library as he was, he was also and
more especially a man of the theater. He went
to the play almost every night, for more than
forty years. He loved the stage; and he expected it to provide him with the particular
pleasure that only the stage can provide. He
had evolved for his own use a body of doctrine
about the drama, derived from his own observations in the theater, but supported by
what he found in Aristotle and in Lessing, who
were both of them men of the theater, as well
as men of the library. As Sarcey was a Frenchman of culture he was an inheritor of the Latin
tradition of form and order, proportion and
harmony.

Much as I admire Sarcey, and much as I
have profited by his analysis of the principles of
playmaking, I have to admit that he "abounded
in his own sense," and that he was overemphatic
in expressing his liking for the "well-made play,"
meaning thereby the pieces of Scribe, of the collaborators who encompassed Scribe about, and
of the disciples of Scribe who were perpetually
producing plays, full of theatrical tricks and
barren of ideas. There never was a more fertile,

more ingenious, more inventive master of mechanism than Scribe. No playwright ever lived who could more artfully get out of a situation all possible theatrical effect. But if Scribe was a master playwright, he was only infrequently a dramatist with a clear vision of life, with the power of creating characters which etched themselves into the memory, and with the sincerity and imagination needful for the larger and nobler types of drama. In almost all the plays of Scribe, the characters are no more than parts for performers; they are realized only in so far as the situations reveal them; and while we may recall for a little space the most striking of his situations, the persons who figure in a play of his fade out of our memories almost immediately. That is to say, a piece by Scribe, or by any of his myriad imitators, is a plot and nothing more, partly because this plot is so elaborated and so complicated that it is sufficient unto itself, and partly because it has no room inside of its intricate mechanism for any genuine projection of humanity. His plays were not unliterary and unimportant because they were "well made" but because they were only clever contrivances, combinations of airless intricacies.

Scribe does not stand alone in his reliance on this combination of invention and construction.

He had predecessors aplenty. Shakspere is one
of them, and Molière is another. Consider the
'Étourdi,' a brisk and bustling farce, carried off
with the high spirits of youthful gaiety, peopled
by stage-types and not by recognizable human
beings. It pleases solely by its swift succession
of laughable situations, all brought about by
a single arbitrary characteristic of the central
figure. It is devoid of ideas; it does not hold
the mirror up to nature; it is not a criticism of
life; it makes us laugh but it does not make us
think after we have laughed. Or consider the
'Comedy of Errors,' one of the earliest of Shakspere's plays as the 'Étourdi' is one of the earliest of Molière's. It is also a succession of vari-
ants of a single situation, the mistaking of one
person for another. It is built up with a deft-
ness and a certainty which Scribe himself might
appreciate. But its adroitly articulated skeleton
is not clothed with flesh and blood; it exists for
its own sake; and it is only toward the end,—
when the mistakes of identity cause the faithful wife to fear that her husband is faithless—
that we can detect "the ruddy drop of human
blood," which is the elixir of life.

Neither the 'Comedy of Errors' nor the
'Étourdi' ranks high in the list of their authors'
works; and the fame of Shakspere and of Molière would be little diminished if these two

pieces had not survived. Yet if they are negligible in themselves they are significant in that they disclose an early acquisition of technical skill. It was because Shakspere had labored loyally in putting together the factitious plot of the 'Comedy of Errors' that he was able later to achieve the solid framework of 'Othello,' just as Molière's hard work in devising the lively story of the 'Étourdi' enabled him later to erect the superb structure of 'Tartuffe.' The 'Comedy of Errors' and the 'Étourdi' are only "well-made plays," whereas 'Othello' and 'Tartuffe' are plays so marvelously well made that the spectators yield themselves to the emotional appeal without giving a thought to the means whereby it is potent over their sympathies.

II

IN our awakened relish for the portrayal of our common humanity and in our exasperated reaction against merely theatrical contrivances, there is danger that we may go too far and be tempted to neglect the art of construction and even to despise it. And that way madness lies. There are ignorant and arrogant youngsters in all the arts, who shout aloud their abhorrence of technic, and who do not understand what Stevenson meant when he implored all artists to master its mysteries:

Think of technic when you rise and when you go to bed. Forget purposes in the meanwhile; get to love technical processes; to glory in technical success; get to see the world entirely through technical spectacles, to see it entirely in terms of what you can do. Then, when you have anything to say, the language will be apt and copious.

When you have anything to say! The trouble with Scribe is, not that he thought too much of technic, but that he had nothing to say. And the trouble with not a few of those who have something to say, is that they have never learned how to say it. Not having served an arduous apprenticeship, they cannot hope ever to achieve a masterpiece. Because they have not wrestled strenuously with the difficulty of putting together a 'Comedy of Errors' or an 'Étourdi,' they have not acquired skill to construct an 'Othello' or a 'Tartuffe.' They are not only deficient in craftsmanship but they do not desire to attain it. A novice in story-telling asked one of my colleagues to read a little tale; and when this youngster was told by his elder that his narrative was rather formless, he retorted proudly, "but form is just what we are trying to get rid of!"

The formless play, the mere succession of

"slices of life" is not the new thing which the French Naturalists of forty years ago vaunted it to be. It is not the latest development of the drama; in fact, it is to be found in the infancy of the art. While the supreme tragedies of the Attic dramatists are beautifully built, there are not a few of their less successful plays which are straggling in structure, with a story unified only by the continuous presence of the protagonist in scene after scene. More than two thousand years ago, Aristotle exprest his disapproval of the tragedies which were loosely put together; and Aristotle knew what he was talking about. Like Lessing later, and like Sarcey also, he derived his theories from his own observations in the theater itself; he did not deduce them out of his inner consciousness as the Italian criticasters were to do in the Renascence. He declared that a drama should have an action "that is complete and whole" with a beginning, a middle and an end, an action neither beginning nor ending at haphazard. And he poured scorn upon the piece which was only a string of slices of life. "Of all plots and actions the episodic are the worst; I call a plot *episodic* in which the episodes or acts succeed one another without probable or necessary sequence." The case for the solidly built play could not be more conclusively stated.

When we recall how the tragedy of the Greeks was directly descended from an artless piece which presented successive moments in the career of a demigod, we have no cause for surprise that even the masters of tragedy did not always strive to stiffen the story with a controlling purpose and to unify the plot into harmonious singleness. Rather may we wonder how it was that Æschylus was able to bestow its massive momentum on his 'Agamemnon,' and how Sophocles could climb to the austere height of his 'Œdipus the King.'

Like Athenian tragedy, English tragedy was developed from popular plays—those which had sprung up spontaneously in the later Middle Ages. So it is that we find the episodic piece, the chronicle-play or history like 'Henry V,' preceding the true tragedy like 'Macbeth,' just as the 'Persians' had preceded 'Agamemnon.' In the chronicle-play the episodes succeed one another without "probable or necessary sequence"; and the sole unity is that of the hero himself. In the tragedy, which was slowly evolved out of the chronicle-play (by the influence of the Greeks transmitted through Seneca's rhetorical dialogs), we have an action complete and whole, with a beginning, a middle and an end, an action neither beginning or ending at haphazard.

57

The chronicle-play is a panorama rather than a play. It is not only the earliest kind of piece to be put together, it is also the easiest. And it is perhaps because it is easy that it is continuously attractive to playwrights, even to some who have shown themselves capable of vanquishing the manifold difficulties of logical construction. Shakspere's 'Richard II' is frankly a chronicle-play, in the manner of Marlowe, whereas 'Richard III,' while it is externally a chronicle-play, is almost a true tragedy, because its action is held together and made more dramatic by the slow fulfilment of Queen Margaret's comprehensive curse. So Molière's 'Don Juan' lies, in like manner, midway between chronicle-play and tragedy; it is episodic, but it is not haphazard.

More than one modern playwright has shown his liking for the laxity of the episodic piece, and has been satisfied to revive the chronicle-play with only a few latter-day ameliorations of method. Nearly a century ago the elder Dumas wrote a chronicle-play about Napoleon and more than half-a-century ago Giacometti wrote another about Marie Antoinette. In our own century Mr. John Drinkwater has presented us with an episodic piece about Lincoln and Mr. Bernard Shaw another about Joan of Arc. And those of us who have sat at the feet of Aristotle

58

could not but wish that these two British writers had braced themselves for the arduous labor of a method less openly haphazard and more vigorously artistic. In our enjoyment of a work of art, part of our pleasure is due to our intuitive knowledge that difficulty has been overcome by a master workman who has served his apprenticeship. In the episodic piece, in the chronicle-play, the difficulty is decreased, and so is the pleasure.

III

Scribe's immediate successors in his own country were his pupils, Sardou more openly than Augier or the younger Dumas. In the 'Pattes de Mouche,' in 'Fédora,' and in the 'Tosca' Sardou is a manufacturer of "well-made plays," in which we take what interest we can in watching the wheels go round. But Sardou was more than a mere manufacturer of mechanical toys; he was now and again a satirist girding at the foibles of his fellow Parisians. In the 'Famille Benoiton,' in 'Nos Bons Villageois,' and in half-a-dozen other comedies of modern life, he projected a group of lightly sketched comic figures which he paraded in his first and second acts only to thrust them out of sight when he was ready to deal with the emotional experiences of the hero and the heroine. This type of play, semisatiric, semimelodramatic, is neither fowl or flesh or good red herring; it is a hybrid, which Scribe would have disavowed. What Sardou lacked was artistic conscience. He was a trained historian; he was a born playwright; he had many gifts; but he threw away his birthright for a mess of plottage. Instead of doing the best that was in him, he found his profit in juggling with a bag of tricks. Even in his more ambitious historical plays, 'Patrie,' 'La Haine' and 'Théodora,' he was not bold or straightforward; he put his trust in arbitrary artifices, and he brought about his catastrophes by the long arm of coincidence and not by the finger of fate.

Much as I admire the robust honesty of Emile Augier and the verve and the vigor of the younger Dumas, I must acknowledge that they also went to school to Scribe, even if they were not docile scholars. They learnt from their master how to tell a story on the stage, but they were less preoccupied with the intrigue itself than they were in the human beings they had created to carry it on. They had opinions of their own and wanted to say their say about society as they saw it; and this forced them to diminish the machinery to make room for humanity. As Dumas and Augier grew in power

60

the influence of their teacher is less evident. The 'Demi-Monde' of Dumas has a last act which is strongly reminiscent of Scribe; it is surpassingly clever with a cleverness almost too deliberate. On the other hand, the later 'Francillon,' with a finer wit and an equal mastery of resource, is less consciously ingenious. The 'Gendre de M. Poirier' (in which Augier had Sandeau for a collaborator) is composed with an economy of method and with a veracity of characterization to which Scribe never aspired. The 'Gendre de M. Poirier' throws back to Molière; and it is the finest example in the nineteenth century of the high comedy for which Molière set the pattern in the 'Femmes Savantes.' It is admirably constructed but it is not a "well-made play" in the narrower meaning of the term.

Dumas and Augier began as disciples of Scribe; and in like manner Ibsen began as a disciple of Augier and Dumas; and as they had had to reduce the number of wheels and springs, cogs and pinions, because they needed space for something more important than mechanism, so Ibsen made further reductions because he had even more to say than they had. As they had departed from the formula of Scribe, so Ibsen departed from their formulas, altho he had served his time and learnt his trade under their tutelage. Ibsen's earliest social dramas are imitative in method. The 'League of Youth' has its affinities with the 'Rabagas' of Sardou; and even the 'Doll's House' is only a Scandinavian treatment of a story which might have been laid in France.

The artfully complicated plot unrolled before us in the first two acts, the threat of the blackmailer, the incriminatory letter in the box, the shawl-dance, these all promised the spectators "a well-made play" of the strictest sect; and only in the last act when husband and wife sit at the table opposite to one another to talk over their married life and to discuss the way out of it,—only then, a few minutes before the curtain falls for the last time, is it that Ibsen asserts himself and casts aside his Gallic disguise. If Scribe had been called upon to edit the 'Doll's House,' we may be sure that he would have grabbed a blue pencil to cancel this marital conversation in order to bring about a happy ending which would have falsified the meaning of the play.

What Scribe would have done to 'Ghosts' it is impossible to conjecture. In that somber and implacable tragedy, there is no trace of the "well-made play." As Augier in the 'Gendre de M. Poirier' throws back to Molière, so Ibsen in 'Ghosts' throws back to Sophocles. In the

Scandinavian play as in the Greek, there is a ghastly story handled with unrelenting firmness. An appalling situation is set before us, with stark austerity; and the long chain of terrible happenings which are the causes remote and immediate of this awful climax are revealed, one by one, only as the grim tragedy draws to its inexorable and inevitable end. What Ibsen does in 'Ghosts' is what Sophocles had done in 'Œdipus the King'; he gives us only a tensely compacted fifth act, moving as irresistibly as an avalanche. No higher tribute could be paid to the constructive skill of Ibsen than to compare it with that of Sophocles. 'Ghosts' and 'Œdipus the King' are supreme examples of the art of dramatic construction, surpassing in dramaturgic dexterity even 'Othello' and the 'Alcalde of Zalamea,' 'Tartuffe' and 'Phèdre'—all of them so securely built that the spectators never suspect the labor which went to the laying of the solid foundation or to the erection of the hidden steel frame. Here we have the art which conceals art,—a refinement which we never find in the "well-made play." These masterpieces are so well made that our attention is not called to the methods of their making. Good cooks do not print the recipe on the bill of fare.

63

IV

I FEAR me greatly that what I have here written may seem to some readers unduly argumentative, since nobody denies what I have sought to prove; and I shall be sorely grieved if I seem to have robbed the katydid of its privilege of saying "the undisputed thing in such a solemn way." But is this thing undisputed? I hold it to be indisputable; none the less have I heard it denied by those whose dislike for the complex futility of the "well-made play" has led them to relish "slices of life" which have not been prepared for the table by a master of the craft.

A perplexed student once called my attention to an essay which held up to admiration as an example of Shakpere's skill as a playwright that feeblest of his later pieces, 'Cymbeline,' a play which contains many lovely lines but which has no more backbone than a jelly-fish. Considered simply as a specimen of playmaking it is careless, clumsy, and amorphous; and by reason of these deficiencies it is undramatic. It has never been able to maintain itself on the stage. It is worse than episodic, for its action is both confused and halting.

Aristotle's advice to aspiring playwrights is

as valid to-day as it was twenty centuries ago. The practices of the Athenian dramatists were not those of the Elizabethans, and those of the Elizabethans were not those of the Victorians; but the principles of playmaking abide unchanging through the ages. To-day as in every yesterday that drama is most worthy of success and of survival which is able to arouse and retain and augment the interest of the spectators, when its plot is single, when its action is direct and swift, when its exposition is clear, when it has sustained suspense without disconcerting surprises, when its story moves steadily from its beginning through its middle to its end, when it centers our attention on its essential elements, when it omits all non-essential details, when every situation is prepared for and in its turn prepares us for those that are to follow, when it has proportion and harmony and symmetry, and when, to sum up, it is well and truly made by an honest craftsman who is also a gifted artist.

(1924)

IV

THE QUESTION OF THE SOLILOQUY

IV

THE QUESTION OF THE SOLILOQUY

I

WHENEVER our Juvenile Highbrows are lured into a consideration of mid-Victorian drama, they are likely to denounce it, not because it was unduly theatrical and pitiably barren, but because it bristled with asides and with soliloquies. Whenever one of their diatribes happens to fall under my eye, I wonder why they fail to distinguish between these two devices. They may say what they will against the aside, and I shall not be moved to protest; but when they scoff at the soliloquy, I ask myself if they are not a little too sure, as is the wont of inexperience, that this device dear to our grandfathers is not going to be found useful by our grandchildren. I am inclined to believe that the protest against the soliloquy is shrill only in the mouths of those who write about the theater, and that those who write for the theater are less vocal. Few dramatists to-day dare to let their characters soliloquize; but I doubt if they are all of them convinced that they ought to respect the sentence of death which has been imposed on the soliloquy.

I was confirmed in this dubiety when I recently read an essay on 'Realism on the Stage' by Mr. George Arliss, an accomplished actor who is also a skilful playwright. Mr. Arliss asserted that

the soliloquy has passed away during my own time on the stage; I should say roughly, within the last twenty-five to thirty years. That is generally regarded as a step forward in construction; whether it is, or is not, seems to me open to question. It is true that the soliloquy was artificial; but was it any more so than the thing which has taken its place?

What gives piquancy to Mr. Arliss's question is the fact that he propounded it in an article written at the time when he was impersonating the Rajah of Ruhk in the 'Green Goddess' of William Archer, and while he was at every performance ending the play with a soliloquy. Mr. Arliss was deft in his acting and the audience did not notice that his final speech before the final fall of the curtain was not addressed to any character in the play and was in fact delivered directly to the spectators. I recalled also that Archer (in his stimulating study of the 'Old Drama and the New') had been severe in his strictures on the mid-Victorian playwrights who were given to a clumsy and unintelligent employment of the abhorrent trick; and yet here he was, using this very trick himself,—but so dexterously that he was not caught in the act. And when the soliloquy is utilized with this unobtrusive felicity it justifies itself; and it reveals itself as too useful a device to be discarded merely because bunglers have mis-used it.

I am reminded also that Bronson Howard, a playwright, who was one of the rare artists capable of doing the right thing in the right way and of being able to explain why he had so done it—I recall that Howard once said to me, "I believe so strongly in the necessity of the soliloquy that if I were to write a play without one, I should go over my piece to find a fit place to insert a soliloquy, thus asserting my right to employ it when I needed it!"

When he said this, he was engaged on the last play of his to be produced, 'Peter Stuyvesant, Governor of New Amsterdam' (in which I was his collaborator). As it happens, our play did not contain a single soliloquy,—but it was none the less unsuccessful.

Mr. Arliss admitted that the soliloquy is artificial, that is to say out of nature, not in accord with the facts of life. So is the blank verse of Shakspere, so is the rimed hexameter of Molière, so is the compact prose of Ibsen, so is the room with its fourth wall removed that the spectators may behold the action on the stage, so is the raised voice of the hero when he makes love to the heroine, so are all the other conventions which are necessary to the existence of the drama and to its fullest effect. No author ever risks the prolixity of real life and no actor (if so be he knows his business) ever stands or walks or talks as he would in real life; on the stage he can seem real only by skilfully disguising the unreality imposed on him by the conditions of the theater. I doubt if there ever was an actress who conveyed the impression of absolute veracity more adequately than Duse did; but hers was the essential reality of consummate art, not the reproduction of unpremeditated nature.

No one can deny that the soliloquy is artificial, altho Victor Hugo did attempt a futile defence, alleging that in moments of emotional stress a man is likely to speak aloud. This is true enough; but what a man utters at these moments is, more often than not, "unfit for publication." Hugo's feeble plea does not validate the long soliloquy of the King in 'Hernani,' with its hundred couplets of rimed alexandrines. But, if Hugo's excuse is invalid, is there any other more acceptable? And the answer to this is that there are two different kinds of soliloquy, that for one of them it is difficult to find a good word, and that for the other there is much to be said. The one kind being beyond justification has properly fallen into disrepute; and the other has unfairly suffered for the villainy of its double.

II

In the 'Conférences chez Beaubichon,' a light and lively little farce, acted at the Variétés in Paris in the sixties of the nineteenth century, the scene is laid in the apartment of M. Beaubichon; and when the curtain rises he comes down to the footlights and begins at once to explain the delicate situation in which he finds himself. This opening speech of his is addressed to no one in particular; and he is alone on the stage. When he has put the spectators in possession of all the facts needful for them to apprehend the action of the play, he concludes by remarking that "they say the soliloquy is unnatural. Well, it may be—but just see how convenient it is!" Then another character enters, and the soliloquy is succeeded by dialog.

That is as simple and as frank as the prolog of any one of the plays of Plautus; and the writers of the French farce had not the excuse of the Latin author, since the Parisian audience was not as dull or as illiterate as one mob of freedmen which noisily assembled in the Roman theater. The French collaborators (I think there were three of them) had shown an impudent ingenuity in compacting their exposition into a single speech; and the joke was on the audience, which was willing enough to laugh with them. While these collaborators were franker than was customary sixty years ago, they had precedents for utilizing the soliloquy as the swiftest method of supplying information that the audience needed to have if it was to understand the events about to be set forth. Molière had done it before them, and he had been only following in the footsteps of the Italian performers of improvised comedy. And the Italians had been carrying on the tradition of the medieval drama, in which it was not uncommon for each of the chief characters to name himself and to describe himself at his first appearance on the stage.

This medieval method survives to this day— or did until very recently—in the so-called "mummers' plays," inherited from the middle ages and performed annually in out-of-the-way corners of England. In Mr. E. K. Chambers's solidly documented account of the 'Medieval Stage,' he records that in one of these degenerate dramas the Devil comes before the spectators and immediately informs them who he is:

In comes I, Beelzebub,
On my shoulder I carry my club,
In my hand a wet leather frying-pan;
Don't you think I'm a funny man?

In another of these mummers' plays the speaker of the prolog begins by saying:

Here comes I, Father Christmas, welcome or welcome
not,
I hope Old Father Christmas will never be forgot.

Was it from the mummers' plays, I wonder, that W. S. Gilbert borrowed this device? Certainly he used it in more than one of his merry ballad-operas. Sir Joseph Porter narrates in verse his origin and his rise to power until he has become at last "the ruler of the Queen's Navee." Of course Gilbert did not venture to employ a device as crude as this in those of his plays which were to be said and not to be sung, in 'Sweethearts' for example or in 'Pygmalion and Galatea.' Yet Shakspere had done it as unhesitatingly as Molière. Iago and Richard III when they are alone on the stage talk straight to the spectators, to the gallants on their three-penny stools and to the groundlings standing in the yard. Both of these bold bad characters un-bosom themselves in soliloquy, revealing their dark designs and letting us see into their black hearts.

The reason why no modern playwright would dare to do this is twofold. First, the bare plat-

75

form of the Tudor theater (with a part of the audience seated on the stage and almost touching the performers) has slowly evolved into the picture-frame stage of our twentieth-century playhouses, equipt with scenery, furniture, and properties, all chosen to produce an effect of reality, whereby the actor is admonished not to "get out of the picture," as he would do if he were to come down to the footlights to take the audience into his confidence. A change of theatrical conditions makes imperative a change of dramaturgic methods; and the comfortable theaters of the twentieth century are as unlike as may be to the rude and unroofed playhouses of the early seventeenth century. What was tolerable to our forefathers of three hundred years ago would be intolerable to us to-day, accustomed as we have been gradually to a subtler mode of conveying information.

Then there is a second reason for the disappearance of the explanatory soliloquy; our playwrights are more skilful than their predecessors of the nineteenth, eighteenth, seventeenth, and sixteenth centuries. They may not be equal to their elders in poetic power or in creative imagination, but they are more consciously and more conscientiously artistic in their construction. Archer carries conviction when he asserts that the craftsmanship of to-day is far more expert than the craftsmanship of yesterday. Our modern playwrights recognize the difficulty of solving the intricate and delicate problems of playmaking. They do not take short cuts across lots; rather do they strive, diligently and often successfully, to force stumbling-blocks to serve as stepping-stones. They have the joy of the artist in grappling with technic; and they find their profit,—their artistic profit—in overcoming obstacles which may seem insuperable. Here they are treading the trail blazed by Molière, who did not allow Tartuffe any of the self-revealing soliloquies such as Iago indulges in whenever the spectators needed to be reminded that he is a villain of the deepest dye. Tartuffe never drops the mask of piety even when he is alone; and yet Molière has so ingeniously presented him to us that we know him for what he is—that we know him better than he knows himself.

In other of his comedies Molière is not so scrupulous; and in some of his more farcical comedies he uses the soliloquy for exposition almost as frankly as the authors of the 'Conférences chez Beaubichon' were to do two centuries later. He even goes so far in one play as to let a character who is soliloquizing discover another character about to enter, whereupon he concludes his soliloquy by hoping that the newcomer has not overheard what he has been saying. And Shakspere lets Romeo in the garden below overhear the soliloquy of Juliet in the balcony above.

III

Juliet's soliloquy is not for the purpose of conveying information which the audience needs to have; it has a wholly different purpose; it is to reveal to us the state of the heroine's heart, and to let us know what she is thinking. What she says then when she is alone with the night is what she would not say to any other character in the play; it is too intimate, too sacred for actual conversation. So Hamlet's "To be or not to be" conveys to us the thoughts which were surging in his brain and which could not be conveyed to us unless Hamlet was permitted by the poet to think aloud. These two soliloquies, therefore, of Juliet and of Hamlet are entirely unlike the soliloquies of Iago and Richard III. They are not merely methods of allowing the spectators an insight into the real characters of these two villains, they are windows to the souls of Juliet and of Hamlet at those crises of their several fates. Juliet and Hamlet tell us what they are feeling at the moment, whereas Iago and Richard III express opinions about themselves which it is inconceivable that they should hold, describing themselves as they really are and not as they probably believed themselves to be. So it is that the speeches of Iago and Richard III to the spectators are not thinking aloud as are the speeches of Juliet and Hamlet. Their soliloquies are therefore as false in psychology as they are primitive in dramaturgy.

Professor A. C. Bradley put the case concisely when he told us that "in listening to a soliloquy we ought never to feel that we are being addressed." But the soliloquy in which the character unpacks his heart and lays bare before us his inmost thoughts belongs plainly to a different class from the soliloquy which has been used mainly to convey information. In listening to the one we do not feel that we are being addressed, and in listening to the other we cannot help feeling that the author is talking to us through the mouth of the character. It is the information soliloquy which strikes us nowadays as absurdly artificial, as an artistic anachronism, as a device unworthy of any self-respecting modern dramatist. And it is the thinking-aloud soliloquy which Mr. Arliss regretted, which Archer utilized discretely at the end of the 'Green Goddess' and which Bronson Howard desired to reserve the right to use.

It must be admitted that even the thinking-aloud soliloquy is artificial, that it is "unnatural" in the sense that it is contrary to the facts of every-day life. And what of it? The drama can exist only when it is allowed to depart from the facts of every-day life. These departures we accept without cavil when we go to the play. We accept it without remarking them; and if our attention happens to be called to them, still we accept them because they conduce to our pleasure. We want to understand Hamlet and Juliet and Julius Cæsar, so we want them to speak English, and if the theme is lofty, we want them to speak also in blank verse, the cadence of which enhances our delight.

Now that the picture-frame stage is the only one we know, the information soliloquy has departed, never to return; and there are none so poor as to regret its leaving. But the thinking-aloud soliloquy will be needed whenever there is a revival of the poetic drama, whenever we shall be blessed by the possession of a playwright who is a poet or of a poet who is a playwright. And in the meantime it can be employed without discovery by dramatists as dexterous as William Archer.

(1923)

80

V

ON THE RIGHT OF AN AUTHOR
TO REPEAT HIMSELF

ON THE RIGHT OF AN AUTHOR
TO REPEAT HIMSELF

I

ONCE upon a time—and not so long ago—
I wrote a newspaper article insisting on
the essential distinction between true criticism
and mere book-reviewing. As I had intermit-
tently plied the trade of book-reviewer for more
than fifty years, I had had come to certain con-
clusions about it; and one of them was that
book-reviewing is (and ought to be) journalism,
whereas criticism is (or ought to be) literature,
at least in its intent if not in its execution. Reviewing, as I see it, is reporting on the content
and the quality of a new book for the benefit
of the readers of the periodical, daily or weekly,
monthly or quarterly, in which it appears. The
critic can adventure his soul in contact with
masterpieces, whereas the reviewer has to do
the best he can with the books of the day, few
of which are the work of a master. In other
words, the critic deals mainly with the past,
while the reviewer has perforce to deal with the
present. Since this is the case, the aims and the

methods of the reviewer necessarily differ from those of the critic.

Two or three months after my little essay appeared I chanced to see in another periodical an article expressing sharp dissent from what I had said, asserting dogmatically that book-reviewing is and must be and ought to be criticism, and holding me up to scorn because my little essay was very like a longer article which I had written ten or fifteen years earlier. In fact, the writer of the retort seemed to suggest that I had been guilty of the high crime and misdemeanor of plagiarizing from myself and that I was thereby defrauding the public. That I had repeated myself was something I could not deny; and in the slang of the street, I had been "caught with the goods on me." All I could do was to plead guilty and throw myself on the mercy of the court. I did not dare to call witnesses to my previous good character, because there was danger that one or another of them might, under skilful cross-examination, disclose the damning fact that I had repeated myself on other occasions in discussing other themes.

All I could do to clear myself even in my own eyes was to deny the constitutionality of the law under which my assailant sought to convict me. I went to the root of the matter and asked if there was any enactment prohibiting an author from repeating himself as often as he saw fit? On this ground I felt secure; and I had no difficulty in convincing myself that there was no such law, that there never had been, and that even if it had been enacted it had been violated so persistently and so abundantly by all sorts and conditions of writers that it had become a dead letter, self-repealed by its own absurdity.

Who am I, so that I should set up for myself a standard of literary legality loftier than that attained by the masters at whose feet I have sat to acquire wisdom? Is there any one of these masters, if so be he was spontaneous and affluent, and if also he was granted a revered longevity, who had not repeated himself boldly and frequently? Did not Stevenson smilingly confess that he did not know how often he had written "it was a wonderful night of stars"? Did not Matthew Arnold assert again and again, and yet again, that in his day in Great Britain there was "an upper class materialized, a middle class vulgarized, and a lower class brutalized"? Did not Macaulay perch his fabled New Zealander on a broken arch of London Bridge two or three times in various essays before he left him at last lost in musing contemplation, in the review of Ranke's 'History of the Popes'?

So far had I progressed in my preparation of

85

my brief for the defence, when I bethought me of a passage in the 'Autocrat of the Breakfast Table,' which seemed to me to have almost the sanctity of a unanimous decision by the Supreme Court of the United States. So I here offer it in evidence, as exhibit A:

You don't suppose that my remarks made at this table are like so many postage-stamps, do you—each to be only once uttered? If you do, you are mistaken. He must be a poor creature that does not often repeat himself. Imagine the author of the excellent piece of advice, "Know thyself," never alluding to that sentiment again during the course of a protracted existence! Why, the truths a man carries about with him are his tools; and do you think a carpenter is bound to use the same plane but once to smooth a knotty board with, or to hang up his hammer after it has driven its first nail? I shall never repeat a conversation, but an idea often. I shall use the same types when I like, but not commonly the same stereotypes. A thought is often original, tho you have uttered it a hundred times. It has come to you over a new route, by a new and express train of associations.

And now, after that, I should be greatly surprised if the judges in Special Sessions, overawed by the weight of these precedents or moved more immediately by common sense, did not at once release me from custody and authorize me to leave the court without a stain on my character.

II

THUS restored to liberty and reassured in equanimity, I was about to congratulate myself on my escape from the prison the doors of which I had visioned as yawning to engulf me, when I suddenly found myself smiling and then laughing out loud, at the absurdity of my dissipated fears. Of course, every author has the right to repeat himself and almost every author has found his profit in so doing. In fact, the right to repeat himself is guaranteed to us Americans by the Declaration of Independence; it is an essential element in the "pursuit of happiness." Think for a moment how unhappy authors would be if they were forbidden to say again what they had already said. The right to repeat themselves has been theirs since a time whereof the memory of man runneth not to the contrary, as we lawyers say. Homer began it, when he "smote his bloomin' lyre," and evoked the image of "ox-eyed beautiful Juno" or when he told us how the "swift-footed Achilles" answered back. And Maeterlinck was but abiding by the precedents when after Paul Heyse had refused to authorize the borrowing of a situation from "Maria von Magdala" for use in his "Marie Madeleine" he took it none the

87

less, explaining that as he himself had already employed this situation in two of his earlier plays, he saw no reason why he should not utilize it a third time.

Careless speakers have been heard to assert that "Shakspere never repeats," than which no assertion could be more easily disproved. It is true that Shakspere's thoughts were so abundant and his vocabulary so extensive that we do not often catch him saying the same thing in the same way, as Macaulay did, and Stevenson did, and many another of honorable repute in the world of letters. But Shakspere does repeat situations and he does repeat characters. There is an amateur performance at the end of 'Love's Labor's Lost' and another at the end of the 'Midsummer Night's Dream.' Sheeted ghosts appear to affright villains as they draw to their doom in half-a-dozen of Shakspere's more sanguinary dramas. And Edmund in 'King Lear' is a pale and enfeebled repetition of Iago; and Parolles in 'All's Well that Ends Well' is an even fainter reproduction of Falstaff.

Molière, who is like Shakspere in not a few aspects of his genius, is exactly like him in this. He took his material where he found it, as was his right and his duty, but he often found it in his own earlier works. Three times do we behold a lover's quarrel culminating in a reconciliation. As it happened, Molière died when he was only fifty-one; and this lover's quarrel might have been served up to us a fourth or even a fifth, if only he had survived to the ripe old age of Sophocles, Voltaire, Goethe, and Hugo. Half-a-dozen of Molière's lighter comedies have plots which are almost identical with that of 'Étourdi' at the head of the procession and of the 'Fourberies de Scapin' at the end. And Molière repeated characters even more often than Shakspere and with less variation. What is Scapin but Mascarille in a different costume? Consider the lively and authoritative serving maids, impersonated by Madeleine Bejart, are they not, so to speak, all sisters under their skins?

More than one historian of literature has pointed out that there is a strong family likeness between the heroes of most of the 'Waverly Novels,' pleasant young fellows, all of them, but a little pallid by the side of Dugald Dalgetty and Scott's other more highly colored humorous characters. Lowell went so far—and I protest that I think he was going too far—as to suggest that two of Cooper's outstanding characters, Long Tom Coffin and Natty Bumppo himself, were in fact the same man habited in two different garbs:

He has drawn you one character, tho, that is new,
One wildflower he's plucked that is wet with the dew

Of this prest Western world; and, the thing not to mince,
He has done naught but copy it ill ever since;
His Indians, with proper respect be it said,
Are just Natty Bumppo, daubed over with red,
And his very Long Toms are the same useful Nat,
Rigged up in duck pants and a sou'wester hat
(Tho once in a Coffin, a good chance was found
To have clipped the old fellow away underground).

It is only fair to record that a few lines later in the 'Fable for Critics,' Lowell made amends by paying due meed of praise to the creator of the unforgettable Leatherstocking:

Don't suppose I would underrate Cooper's abilities;
If I thought you'd do that, I should feel very ill at ease;
The men who have given to *one* character life
And objective existence are not very rife;
You may number them all, both prose-writers and
  singers,
Without overrunning the bounds of your fingers,
And Natty won't go to oblivion quicker
Than Adams the parson or Primrose the vicar.

It used to be said of a sadly forgotten contemporary of Scott and Cooper, G. P. R. James, that he had a formula for beginning his long-winded and empty romances, "As night was slowly gathering a solitary traveller might have been seen descending the slope of the Apennines," or the Alps or the Cordilleras or the Grampians, as the case might be. And it was also said, but I fear without warrant, that when James's attention had been called to the monotony of this opening sentence, he varied it in his next tale of adventure by stating that on this occasion two solitary travellers might be seen.

III

LIKE G. P. R. James, Robert Louis Stevenson trod in the trail first broken by Walter Scott; but he was too conscious an artist to repeat an opening sentence—unless perhaps "it was a wonderful night of stars." Where Stevenson was wont to repeat himself was not in words, of which he had an ample store, but in places. Certain spots had a fascination for him, since they seemed so remote and so romantic that each of them cried aloud for employment as the setting of an episode. After writing his enthusiastic essay, 'Memoirs of an Islet,' he made further use of the island of Earraid first as the habitat of the 'Merry Men' and second as the isolated spot whereon the young hero of 'Kidnapped' is temporarily marooned. At every repetition the islet is served up with a different sauce, but the piece of resistance is ever the same; and no lover of Stevenson would wish that he had avoided the repetition, even if we now perceive that he has been caught in the act of plagiarizing from himself.

I have already quoted Maeterlinck's unblushing confession that he had used the same situation in three several plays; and I may add as a corollary that Victor Hugo went further and in his 'Lucrèce Borgia' he used what is practically the same situation three or four times. I have read somewhere that Eugene Scribe, that most prolific of playwrights, was condoled with by a friend on the failure of one of his less important pieces and that Scribe waived aside the proffered sympathy with the remark that even if the piece had not been successful it had a good story,—"so I shall write it over again two or three years from now!"

Scribe may have said this or he may not; but what he declared to be his intention was what the younger Dumas actually did. His thesis-play, the 'Idées de Madame Aubry,' did not please at its first performance and it was soon withdrawn. Dumas was not discouraged; he bided his time; and ten or a dozen years later he wrote another play on the same theme, 'Denise,' and this time more skilfully and more successfully.

In so doing Dumas knew what he was about. The theme he was rehandling in the second play was dear to his heart; and he wanted to have it discussed. But I doubt if Victor Hugo was really aware that in building the plot of

'Lucrèce Borgia' he was guilty of self-repetition at the end of successive episodes. If he had been conscious, I think that he would probably have endeavored to disguise these consecutive borrowings from himself. Maeterlinck, on the other hand, was deliberately warming over his own funeral-baked meats when he used again the situation that Paul Heyse had declined to lend him. Probably the German dramatist thought that he had invented the situation and was proud of his invention. After all, it is a wise situation that knows its own father.

A friend with whom I discussed the practice of self-plagiarism called my attention to the fact that John Webster took over a couplet,—

Glories, like glowworms, afar off shine bright;
But, looked to near, have neither heat nor light,

from the 'White Devil' and inserted it unaltered in the 'Duchess of Malfy,' which was produced a few years later. This can hardly have been done unwittingly; and perhaps the poet, feeling that he needed these two lines in the second play, intended to cut them out of the first piece —and forgot to do it. Or perhaps he did not care, having no hope or expectation that his works would be put under the critical microscope three centuries after his death.

The same friend (and why should I not give

93

him due credit for his amicable aid?—it was Mr. Clayton Hamilton) has called my attention to a deliberate and avowed repetition by one of the masters of English prose, Sir Thomas Brown. At the end of the next-to-last paragraph of his 'Urn Burial' we are told that "if any have been so happy as truly to understand Christian annihilation, ecstasies, exolution, liquefaction, transformation, the kiss of the spouse, gustation of God, and ingression into the divine shadow, they have already had an handsome anticipation of heaven; the glory of the world is surely over, and the earth in ashes unto them." Then at the very end of 'Christian Morals' we are assured that "if, as we have elsewhere declared, any have been so happy, as personally to understand Christian annihilation, ecstasy, exolution, transformation, the kiss of the spouse and ingression into the divine shadow, according to mystical theology, they have already had an handsome anticipation of heaven; the world is in a manner over, and the earth in ashes unto them."

If Sir Thomas had been a public speaker instead of a recluse scholar, he might very well have refrained from the admission that he had made the earlier declaration, for whenever the orator has improvised a felicitous phrase which has proved effective when uttered on the plat-

94

form or the stump, he is tempted to utilize it as often as occasion serves. I have seen it stated that Mr. Bryan had employed the striking figure of the Cross of Gold and the Crown of Silver—striking when heard for the first time, even if unconvincing when considered in cold blood—two or three times before he placed it triumphantly at the climax of the perfervid speech which brought him an unexpected nomination for the presidency. There is wisdom in the remark which Mr. Wilton Lackaye once made to Mr. Augustus Thomas,—that "repartee was often a matter of repertoire." Sheridan once taunted a political opponent with "relying on his memory for his wit and on his imagination for his facts." Surely a speaker or a writer has a right to rely on his memory of his own wit on other occasions. It is a pretty poor witticism which is worn out by one using.

IV

THE stump-speaker has at least this excuse for repeating himself, that he is addressing a different crowd every time he stands and delivers; and that the audience of this evening cannot know what he said to the audience of last evening. The magazine-writer is akin to the stump-speaker in that no magazine goes to the same set of subscribers as another magazine. For myself, I confess frankly that I do not hesitate to use in a contribution to one periodical a turn of phrase which I have earlier employed in a contribution to another periodical. I confess further that this self-repetition has given me a deal of trouble when I have had to go over a group of essays written at different times for different reviews, revising them for publication in a single volume.

In my blameless vanity I have felt that it was always possible for a reader of a book of mine to be so entranced by it as to rush it through at a single sitting; and therefore for the benefit of this possible reader have I striven valiantly —but not always successfully—to eliminate the unbecoming frequency with which I may have said the same thing in the same way. I should not like to be forced to count the number of articles wherein I have had to discuss the dearth of drama in English literature in the mid-years of the nineteenth century and wherein I have asserted that in those decades "the plays of our language which were actable were unreadable and the plays which were readable were unactable." I have an affection for that phrase; it seems to me a good phrase, since it puts the case in a nutshell. But I had rather it did not appear in any one of my volumes of collected criticisms more than twice—or at the most thrice. Even after this phrase has made what ought to be its final appearance in a book of mine, I am afraid that I shall not hesitate to use it in the next paper I happen to write for a magazine. And why not? Is it not my own, to do with as I see fit?

It may be that this recalcitrancy of mine is to be explained by my being a college professor, charged with the duty of lecturing on the same subjects year after year to constantly changing groups of students. As a college professor it is laid upon me to find the best way to arouse the interest of my successive classes, concourses of fortuitous atoms totally differing from year to year; and therefore when I have found exactly the right words to characterize one of the authors I have to discuss, it is not only my privilege to use these words, year after year, it is my bounden duty so to do. Regularly every year for now more than three decades I told my class in American literature that Emerson was the representative of the ideal and that Franklin was the representative of the practical, always adding that when Emerson told us to "hitch our wagon to a star," Franklin was ready "to proffer an improved axle-grease."

There may be danger that the professor will let his lectures become stereotyped, and conse-

97

quently soulless. But he does not know his business and he does not deserve to hold his place, unless he is keenly alive to the impression he is making on his class. If his students are inattentive and listless, he knows whose fault it is. When Henry Ward Beecher was once asked what was the best remedy for a somnolent congregation, he is reported to have said that at Plymouth Church they had a simple remedy. "Whenever one of the ushers discovers anybody asleep, he has orders to go at once to the pulpit and wake up the preacher!"

The preacher is under a disadvantage from which the professor is free; he faces the same congregation year after year, whereas the college instructor has a new audience every fall. But both of them need to be on their guard against undue self-repetition. And they cannot save themselves by the cautious writing of their sermons and their lectures, for in so doing they lose more than they gain. They may gain in literary form but they lose the easy freedom of direct speech, halting it may be, but far more effective in establishing contact with the minds of their hearers. As President Butler once aptly put it, "To read a lecture to a class is to insult the printing-press!"

No, the college professor need not hesitate to say again what he has often said before;

and he can find comfort in a saying attributed
to Agassiz, whom Lowell once declared to be
the greatest teacher ever connected with Har-
vard. I have not been able to run down the
time and place of Agassiz' confession nor can I
now recall his exact words; but he had occasion
once to speak of his first lecture in Switzerland,
a lecture expected to fill the canonical hour. At
the end of forty-five minutes he had told his
hearers all he knew, so for the final fifteen minutes he had to repeat himself. Then he added:
"And that is what I have been doing ever since,
—repeating myself."

V

As I reread what I have here written I wonder
whether I have not been abusing the privilege
I claimed. So I refrain from further dilation
upon this tempting topic; and I ask leave only
to make one further quotation. John Hollingshead was for years the manager of the Gaiety
Theater in London. He had begun his career
as a contributor to magazines, as a miscellaneous
writer for all sorts of periodicals; and he explained that he had abandoned the craft of
writing only when he discovered that the man
of letters was like an organ-grinder, in that he
could play only half-a-dozen tunes. When

those had been heard, he had to move to another street and play them over again until he himself got tired of hearing them interminably repeated.

There is a bitter truth in this comparison, I fear; but there was one thing that Hollingshead did not take into account. As the taste in tunes shifts and changes, it is always possible for the organ-grinder to procure a new barrel with another half-dozen tunes.

(1923)

VI

SECOND-HAND SITUATIONS

VI

SECOND-HAND SITUATIONS

I

THERE was published a few years ago a set of four comely little tomes containing nearly twoscore 'Masterpieces of Mystery'; and in the volume devoted to detective stories, I found Poe's 'Purloined Letter' and Sir Arthur Conan Doyle's 'Scandal in Bohemia.' As it happened I was not familiar with the latter; and I read it with increasing surprise as I turned page after page and noted that it was an obvious imitation of the former. Almost up to the very end the stories are essentially the same in theme and in treatment. There is a compromising document—in the first a letter and in the second a photograph—the production of which would create a great scandal in a royal family. The possessor keeps it where it can be instantly produced; and yet it could not be found by the most assiduous search of the possessor's residence. So appeal is made to Dupin in Poe's tale and to Sherlock Holmes in Doyle's. To discover the whereabouts of the document they make use of devices so similar as to justify their being termed identical. M. Dupin finds what he is seeking; and Sherlock Holmes, after ascertaining where it is, finds himself tricked at the very moment of his triumph. Probably it was this ingenious variation from the original which tempted Sir Arthur to his exhibition of this sincerest form of flattery.

In another volume of this same series, devoted to ghost stories, I was glad to reread the 'Horla' of Guy de Maupassant and I was again reminded of its likeness to the 'What was It?' of Fitzjames O'Brien, the most thrilling of the half-dozen brilliantly ingenious tales of that Irish-American story-teller; and I doubt if I am overbold in venturing to think that I may be able to suggest an explanation of the similarity between these two tales of terror. O'Brien imagined a creature invisible but tangible; and he made his readers feel the intensifying fright of the man who slowly becomes conscious of the existence of this monster and who is forced into association with it. 'What was It?' was published anonymously sixty years ago in an American magazine; and forty years ago a British magazine published anonymously what was plainly a plagiarism from it. Yet as I was informed at the time by a friend of the British writer, the plagiarism was unconscious and comparatively innocent, because the apparent plagiarist had received the outline of the story one evening in a club smoking-room from a chance acquaintance who had picked it up he did not know where.

I am inclined to believe that Maupassant also received the notion—as Kipling would call it—from one of his friends. Maupassant did not read English; and he was in the habit of making his profit out of anecdotes and incidents collected for him by his intimates. The 'Pearl Necklace' was based on an actual happening; Marcel Prévost is said to have supplied the material out of which the 'Sisters Rondoli' is made; and we have been made acquainted with the original of the self-sacrificing 'Boule-de-Suif.' As Maupassant utilizes only the main idea of O'Brien's story and does not copy its succession of episodes, he may very well have got it from somebody who had read, not the American original, but the British imitation. But wherever Maupassant got it, he made it his own by adding the appalling suggestion that the invisible companion was possessed of a stronger will than the man he was haunting and that he was hypnotizing his victim. The 'Horla,' it must be remembered, was written toward the end of Maupassant's brief career, when he was obsessed by those hallucinations of persecution which were at last to land him in an asylum.

That Fitzjames O'Brien deserves credit for the original invention is indisputable; and I happen to know that the writer responsible for the publication of the imitation in the British magazine was a man of high character who had never read the American story and who had never heard O'Brien's name. So far as I am aware neither the American original nor the British plagiarism was ever translated into French. Yet the bare outline of the story may have got into oral tradition, so to speak; and it may have passed from mouth to mouth before it reached Maupassant just at that period of his ill-starred career when its eery weirdness would be most appealing to him. Only professional writers of fiction are conscious how often it is that the seed of a story is discovered by the eye in a newspaper or deposited in the ear by a chance conversation.

The pathetic anecdote out of which 'Evangeline' was developed was told at the same time to Hawthorne and Longfellow. Hawthorne announced that he intended to make a story of it; yet so long did he postpone the writing of it, that Longfellow asked him to surrender it for the more poetic investiture it invited. But suppose that both Hawthorne and Longfellow had gone to work, unknown to each other, and had published the result of their labors almost simultaneously, one in prose and the other in verse; there might have arisen a bitter controversy, if not between the two authors who had been classmates at Bowdóin, at least between the special adherents of the one and the special adherents of the other.

II

In the remote days when I was myself a teller of tales I had an alluring notion for a short story, altho I do not now recall whether I had invented it or derived it from something heard or read. Here it is, in the barest statement. The secretary of a very rich man is in love with his employer's only daughter and she with him. She waits for him to declare himself, and this his false pride in his poverty prevents him from doing. They are all on a yacht which is shipwrecked; and as the boat is about to make its last lurch into the ocean, the girl is irresistibly moved to tell him that she loves him and that she knows he loves her. She makes this confession only because she believes that their last hour has come and that they can be united in their impending death. But they are rescued almost miraculously. And try as I would, I could not find a way out of this novel situation, at least none that I could accept as a satisfactory solution. So I gave it up; and one day I told it to Thomas Bailey Aldrich, explaining why I could not use it. He saw its effectiveness and he expressed a belief that he could devise a satisfactory conclusion. I made him a present of my notion and he called the tale he wrote 'Her Dying Words.' But suppose that Aldrich had got this plot from some one of our common friends to whom I may have outlined it and who had omitted to tell him that it came from me. And suppose that we had both written it up and that our rival versions had appeared in rival magazines the same month. I think we should each of us have had an unhappy quarter of an hour.

It was in those distant fiction-writing days of mine that I had another idea, not a plot this time but only a title,—the 'Parrot that Talked in his Sleep.' That seemed to me then, as indeed it does now, to be an enticing title. Unfortunately I could never fit a plot to it. So I offered it in turn to three of my friends, H. C. Bunner, Frank R. Stockton and Rudyard Kipling. Bunner thought up several strange tales for this somnolent bird to figure in; but unfortunately no one of them was quite decorous enough for the Puritan austerity of nineteenth-century taste. Stockton told me that he would see if he could not evolve the matter-of-fact whimsicality which the title foreshadowed. And Kipling said: "Let me have it! Our parrots in India do talk in their sleep!" But as yet that story has not got itself written. Suppose however that Kipling and Stockton, Bunner and I had each of us been unexpectedly visited by the muse and that four different magazines had simultaneously printed tales, differing in content but agreeing in title—the 'Parrot that Talked in his Sleep'—well, stranger things than that have happened and the consequences thereof have been strange indeed.

It must be forty years ago that Andrew Lang sat next me at a luncheon-table in the Savile Club, and told me that Rider Haggard had called upon him that morning full of delight in a highly original notion for a story, a theme which had dawned upon him in the silent watches of the previous night. When this sudden inspiration had been expounded Lang asked Haggard if he had read a just published story by F. Anstey; and when Haggard replied that he knew nothing of it, Lang had to inform him that Anstey's story contained almost exactly the sequence of situations which Haggard believed to be due to his own midnight invention. Here two explanations are possible. The first is that Haggard may have carelessly glanced through a review of the Anstey book and that his memory played him false, leading him to believe that what he remembered had been originated in his own brain. And the other is that he was the victim of one of those coincidences, unusual and inexplicable, which do occur now and again and which resemble the almost simultaneous discovery of the same scientific law by Darwin and by Wallace.

In most cases where we find the same situation used by several writers in succession there has been borrowing,—and if this borrowing is conscious, it must be stigmatized as plagiarism. I am reminded of one such case by finding among these 'Masterpieces of Mystery' a short story of Wilkie Collins's, called 'A Terribly Strange Bed.' As I read it again I thought that it did not justify its inclusion in any series of masterpieces. I should call it a fairly well-told tale, mechanical in its construction and arid in its atmosphere. It sets forth the misadventure of a man who has to sleep in a strange bed in a strange house, a huge bed with four heavy posts supporting a thick canopy. The man discovers in time that this canopy is slowly descending upon him and that he will surely be smothered if he does not roll out. When I read the story first many years ago I had recognized this deadly couch as an old friend, since I had already seen it at work in a melodrama called the 'Maison du Baigneur' written by Auguste Maquet, the collaborator of Dumas in the 'Three Guards-men' and in 'Monte Cristo.' And I have since met with the same murderous contrivance in a short story of Joseph Conrad's.

Now, the easiest explanation of the appearance of this strange bed first in a French play and then in two British tales, one after the other, is that Wilkie Collins (who was a constant playgoer and who was not an infrequent visitor to Paris) had simply annexed it from Maquet, and that Conrad had taken it over either direct from the Frenchman or indirectly from his British predecessor. But on reflection I am not so sure that this explanation is as solid as it is simple. If, as is quite possible, a bed of this ingenious deadliness had actually been invented and used by some professional assassin, then it may be preserved to this day in some collection of gruesome antiquities along with the Iron Maiden and other implements of torture. Or even if it has not actually survived, the record of its employment somewhere and somewhen may exist in the archives of crime. In either case the existence of this fatal instrument as a fact would permit any number of authors to make use of it in fiction. Facts are not only stranger than fiction, but they are common property, free to all, and those who utilize them are innocent of evil intent. There can be no copyright in an actual happening. So it is possible, altho I doubt if it is probable, that Wilkie Collins and Conrad would be justified in putting in a plea of confession and avoidance.

III

It is a fact, or at least it is a legend which got itself incorporated in the contemporary chronicles, that Katherine Douglas, Katherine of the Sea, won her nickname 'Kate Bar-lass' because when the bar which fastened the door was missing, she held the door against rude intruders by thrusting her arm through the staples. There may have been a contemporary ballad in her honor; and her self-sacrificing courage has been commemorated for modern readers in Rossetti's narrative lyric, the 'King's Tragedy.' I think the episode is also to be found in one of Scott's 'Tales of a Grandfather,' and I have been informed that it appears in John Galt's 'Spae Wife.' What I should like to know is where the elder Dumas happened upon it, for it reappears in his 'Henri III,' which was first acted in 1829. (Galt's novel had been published in 1823.) If Dumas got it from the fact, from an historical record, he had every right to make it his own; but if he got it from fiction, from Scott or Galt,—well, in that case he was doing only what he had done before and was to do again, —he was plowing with another man's heifer. Less than a score of years later this effect turned up again in George Lippard's American historical romance, 'Blanche of Brandywine'; and it helped to give an ephemeral popularity to the play which was promptly made out of the novel. And then after a lapse of another score of years it turned up once more in the vigorous melodrama, 'Davy Crockett,' which Frank Murdoch wrote for Frank Mayo, with the transferal to the hero of the heroic feat. Did Lippitt and Murdoch reinvent this effect, either or both of them, or did they borrow it from Dumas, or Galt or Scott? Or did they, like Rossetti, derive it from the chronicle? I confess that I doubt their reinvention of an effect so singular and so striking, and I am inclined to think it more probably that they both took it over, one after the other, from Dumas.

IV

I HAVE elsewhere called attention to the world-wide wonderings of two other effective situations, which travelled from author to author and from country to country, undeterred even by the voyage across the Atlantic. One of them started on its travels in Paris in an opera and in time traversed the English Channel to live again in one of the noblest of historical novels. Thackeray never wrote a scene of more dramatic power than that in which Henry Esmond breaks his sword before the Prince whom he has served loyally and who has proved himself unworthy of this devotion. A scene almost exactly the same is to be found in the 'Twenty Years After' of Dumas, where we see Athos break his sword before Louis XIV. And the same scene had earlier appeared in the opera of the 'Favorite,' for which Donizetti composed the score to a book by Alphonse Royer and Gustave Vaez. Perhaps these two playwrights were the originators of this situation; but as it is known that their libretto had been revised by Eugène Scribe, it is quite possible that the invention ought to be ascribed to him.

The other situation started on its long voyage here in the United States, to make two appearances in Great Britain and then to turn up in India. In the last of Cooper's Leatherstocking tales, the 'Prairie,' Natty Bumppo dies; he has been a soldier and he hears a roll-call inaudible to any of those who stand beside him; he straightens himself, answers "Here!" and falls back dead. In Thackeray's 'Newcomes' the worn-out old colonel sheltered in the Charterhouse where he had been a schoolboy, hears an inaudible roll-call, straightens himself, answers "Adsum!" and falls back dead. In one of Sir Walter Besant's pleasant romances there is an old sailor at the point of death; he draws himself up, salutes, says "Come on board, sir!" and falls back dead. In one of Kipling's early tales of India there is a broken scholar, sodden with opium, who stiffens himself to reply to an unheard question "Not guilty, my lord!" and "the stupor held him till he died."

How are we to account for the reappearance of this effect? Thackeray was a great admirer of Cooper; and he is on record as holding that Leatherstocking was a more acceptable hero than any of "Scott's lot." Quite possibly he did not know that he was repeating an effect of Cooper's. Quite possibly Besant, who was certainly acquainted with the novels of both Cooper and Thackeray, also did not realize that he was using a device they had already employed; and quite possibly again he did know it and believed that he had a right to use it if he varied it as he did. When I asked Kipling if he had been a deliberate borrower, he told me frankly that he had no clear recollection on the point; he was familiar with these stories of all three of his predecessors in the art of fiction, yet he doubted if his death-bed had been suggested by any of them. It deserves to be noted that Kipling's variation of the effect is even more marked than Besant's.

I was discussing this topic once with a small group of graduate students; and I made bold to tell them that this death-bed scene had now been used so often that it had ceased to belong to anybody, that it was common property, and that if any one of them wanted to make a fit end for a character it would be permissible to supply him with a similar last dying speech and confession.

"Then I think I'll write up the death-bed of an elevator-boy," remarked a student; "and of course he would say 'going *down?*' "

On another occasion, not at a conference with students, but at a luncheon attended by half-a-dozen men of letters, I propounded the theory that the first writer who uses a situation deserves credit as its inventor; the second is a plagiarist; the third is merely lacking in originality; and the fourth is only drawing from the common stock.

"Yes," said President Butler, who was sitting opposite to me, "and when the fifth man uses that situation, it's research!"

V

ANY one whose observation is alert and whose memory is retentive will have little difficulty in multiplying examples of what may be called the transmigration of situations. But so far as I can now recall no one of the theatrical reviewers who have had to weigh and to measure the technic of William Archer's skilfully built melodrama, the 'Green Goddess,' has undertaken to trace the ancestry of a device by means of which the adroit dramatist has been able to bring about the most thrilling moment of his fourth and final act. The heroine and the man she loves are captives of the ruthless Rajah of Ruhk, in his palace hidden in the depths of the Himalayas. They are awaiting execution at the hands of the fanatical natives; and they have no expectation of rescue, as they believe that the wireless message they tried to send was not sent. Then, when they have only a few scant minutes to live, the heroine listens intently and cries out that she can hear the drumming of an airplane. A cry like hers had sprung from the lips of the Highland lass who was the heroine of Dion Boucicault's 'Jessie Brown; or the Relief of Lucknow.' The beleaguered British are making their last stand against the Sepoys; they

117

are resolved to sell their lives dearly but they have no hope of succor. Then Jessie Brown calls out, "Dinna ye hear the pipes?" and in a few seconds a Scots regiment takes the Sepoys in the rear.

Boucicault's play was produced more than sixty years ago; and more than fifty years ago J. J. McCloskey's 'Across the Continent' had had for its sensation-scene the siege of a little company of whites in a railroad-station on the plains. The Red Skins had cut the telegraph-wires,—and yet at the tensest moment the whistle of a locomotive is heard, and then a train rushes in, filled with soldiers. And more than twenty years ago a similar situation was utilized with equal effectiveness in David Belasco's 'Girl I Left Behind Me.'

In employing this situation in the 'Green Goddess,' Archer was neither inventor nor plagiarist; he was only drawing from the common stock. He was providing himself with what he needed by a draft on the property-room which the numberless playwrights of the past have richly furnished for the benefit of the playwrights of the present. Only a very young investigator is now venturesome enough to raise the puerile outcry of plagiarism whenever he discovers in a new play a device, an effect, a situation which he chances to recognize as something that he can recall in an older play. It was only the smartness of juvenility which permitted the definition of a plagiarist as "a writer of plays."

There are plagiarists who are writers of plays, no doubt; there always have been and there always will be. In fact, some of the most pro-lific playwrights have been unable to clear them-selves of this charge, the elder Dumas, for one, and Sardou, for another; but it is only fair to point out that these two dramatists, even if now and again they were caught with their hands in the pockets of earlier authors, had always a comfortable balance in the bank, that is to say, they were also and beyond all ques-tion inventors of persistent originality, from whom their contemporaries and their successors have often borrowed.

Moreover, we never know, and perhaps even some of those who are apparently convicted of plagiarism do not know, whether the accusation is or is not well founded. In the trial of these cases, circumstantial evidence is all we have on which to base a verdict; and circumstantial evidence is often misleading. A dramatist may have deliberately helped himself to a situation he needed; or he may have taken it over entirely unconscious that he was drawing on his memory and not on his imagination; or he may, as a matter of fact, have actually reinvented it, not knowing that it had already been invented by some one else.

Perhaps I can here offer myself as a witness. I once wrote a one-act play called 'This Picture and That'; and I did not doubt that I had originated the central situation. But a little later I was shocked to find it in Bronson Howard's 'Henrietta,' and I noted that Howard had scrupulously acknowledged on the playbill that he was indebted for it to 'Vanity Fair.' Of course, I had read Thackeray's novel; I had read it two or three times, perhaps oftener, and therefore I am unable to say whether or not I had unconsciously borrowed. Again, I once wrote a short story called 'Her Letter to his Second Wife,' in which a wife who knew that she was dying penned an epistle of advice to her unknown successor. After my tale was published I was informed that a similar letter of conjugal counsel existed in a short story written by William Allen White. I do not happen to know which of our stories had first got into print; I believe that it was White's; but I had not only not read it, I was absolutely unaware of its existence.

After all, the many stories of business life in America, in which the poor young hero falls in love with his rich boss's daughter and is ultimately rewarded with her hand—these popular tales with essential sameness in theme and with infinite variety in working out, cannot all of them be plagiarisms from Hogarth's 'Industrious Apprentice.'

(1920)

VII

CLAPTRAP

VII

CLAPTRAP

I

IN the good old days, more than half-a-century ago, when almost every theater in the United States had a resident stock company, changing its membership slowly and often enduring substantially the same season after season, the actor was engaged on a weekly salary with the privilege of "taking a benefit" one night in the two or three weeks before the house closed for the summer. The proceeds of this special performance he shared with the manager in a proportion agreed upon in the contract; and he was allowed to arrange the program of the evening to suit himself. Naturally, he chose plays in which he could display to advantage his own ability; and he was able often to "strengthen the cast" by inviting the participation of popular performers not connected with the company.

A benefit performance was an almost certain gage of the esteem in which the actor was held by the community in which he had practised his art for months and in some cases for years. Of course, the most profitable benefits were

those of the performers of the dashing heroes
and the lovelorn heroines, to whom the sympathy of successive audiences had gone out
superabundantly. Next in rich return was the
night of the low comedian whose merry voice
heard off stage always evoked a smile of an-
ticipatory enjoyment. Sometimes even the
"heavy man," who was hissed night after night
as a villain of the deepest dye, was so powerful
an actor that he had impressed his personality
upon persistent playgoers, or, at least, upon
enough of them to fill the house comfortably
when his name was put up.

But there was only a slim chance of a profitable benefit for the less important members
of the company, the undistinguished subordi-
nates, faithful enough, but subdued to what
they worked in and aptly characterized by the
name of their line of business—"responsible
utilities." How could a performer of utility-
parts, appearing only in a scene or two, and
even then saying little and doing less to focus
attention upon himself,—how could he hope
to acquire a popularity ample enough to attract a throng to his benefit? The solution of
this problem must have vext the soul of many
a performer of responsible utilities, well aware
that very few of the spectators were acquainted
even with his name; and many an ingenious

expedient must have been devised in the vain hope of dispelling the obscurity which necessarily shrouded the individuality of those who impersonated only insignificant characters.

One of these expedients, preserved in oral tradition, has so descended to me (altho for all I know it may have got itself recorded in print). Three or four score years ago, so runs the tale, as the season was drawing to an end at the Bowery Theater, there was performed an old-fashioned melodrama, compounded of intrigue and mystery and murder; and as the fourth of its five acts drew toward a climax, a utility-man rushed on the stage to deliver the letter of dire import for which the distracted hero had been waiting.

"This—from the King!" cried he, as he bent low and handed the missive to the leading man. Then he drew himself up, marched down to the footlights and raised his voice to be heard of all men. "Let me add that he who lays his hand upon a woman, save in the way of kindness, is unworthy to be called an American!"

Cheers rent the air at this noble sentiment. The utility-man bowed in response and backed himself off the stage through the nearest exit.

When at last the curtain fell on the act, the leading man, anger blazing in his eye and wrath burning in his voice, bore down upon the utility-man and asked what he meant by ruining the big scene of the play.

"Well," said the culprit, unrepentant and unabashed, "I've got a benefit to take care of just as you have!"

I am inclined always to distrust the tales that lead a hand-to-mouth existence, unauthenticated in chapter and verse; and this anecdote may be apocryphal. Yet it has its value; and it is only one of many. Nor is the humble utility-man alone in his appeal to patriotism. Another anecdote, perhaps more trustworthy, since it has attached itself to an actor whose name has come down to us,—has to do with one Kirby, a performer of fiery robustious parts. He appeared as the hero of a war-play, dangerously wounded while battling bravely in behalf of his country, whereupon he called out to his valiant comrades in arms, "Wrap me in the American flag, and let me die!"

As it happens, I can draw from my own store of theatrical reminiscences an unexcelled example of this overpowering assault upon patriotic prejudice. Nearly half-a-century ago, when Drury Lane was under the management of Augustus Harris, I had the privilege of beholding upon its venerable boards a highly colored drama, intricate in plot, swift in action, absorbing in interest, rich in sensational scenes, and in fact artfully compounded to delight the unthinking crowd. It was stage-managed by Harris, who was a past master of the art as it was then understood. It was composed by Harris, in collaboration with Paul Merritt or Henry Pettitt, I forget which; they were both adroit manufacturers of stirring situations and mellifluous sentiment. And the part of the ultra-heroic hero was reserved by Harris for his own acting; he was not a good actor but he was an old stager who knew all the tricks of the trade.

The story of the piece has long since evaporated from my memory, yet I can still sharply visualize the last scene of the next to the last act. A little detachment of British troops has been cut off and is about to be surrounded by fanatic Arabs—the place was Egypt, of course, and the time was that of Arabi Pasha. If succor does not arrive speedily, the British must put up a hopeless fight, dying to the last man. The one chance is that a messenger can make his way through the encircling enemies and notify the general in command of the main body of the army. It is a very slim chance, since the bearer of the missive will be facing almost certain death. Of course, Harris volunteers; he bids farewell to his friends; he disappears over the hastily thrown up parapet. The plot and the subplot and the comic underplot fill up time; and then the Arabs begin their attack. The beleaguered British beat off the first assault; they even manage to repulse the second onslaught; but their ranks are so sadly thinned that they cannot hope to withstand the third rush. There is a moment of dread suspense; and then the Arabs break down the British defences and pour in through the breach. When all seems to be lost there is a sudden bugle-call, heard above the din of combat. It is repeated more loudly; and then the Arabs turn about to repel the rescuers, who now charge almost to the center of the stage, these rescuers captained by the heroic Harris, who posed in the forefront as the curtain falls. At the imperious insistence of tumultuous applause the curtain rises again and the battle is resumed. An Arab bullet strikes the standard-bearer, but Harris is there to catch the flag from the loosening grasp of the dying man. And the curtain falls once more with Harris holding on high the Union Jack. A second time it rises, and again the battle rages, but only for a moment, as a stray shot soon wounds Harris, who staggers forward, clasping the flag to his breast and at last falling only a few feet from the footlights. And when the actors passed before the curtain one after another Harris came last of all, still clutching the standard.

II

MORE than two centuries ago the users of the English language felt the need of a fit word to describe a thing of this sort; and as usual the word-making faculty of the English-speaking race was equal to the occasion. In a dictionary printed in 1727 we find *claptrap* defined as "a trap to catch a clap by way of applause from the spectators at a play." More than a hundred years later Southey, in one of his letters, almost foresees the trickery of the Harris curtain picture,—"there will be no claptraps, nothing about 'Britannia rules the waves.'"

The illustrative quotations in other dictionaries trace the swift passage of this useful word from the theater to the forum. Brougham asserted that Sheridan in his political speeches "played to the galleries and indulged them, of course, with an endless succession of claptraps"; and Herbert Spencer in his 'Study of Sociology' asked us to "observe how votes are gained by claptrap appeals to senseless prejudices." Here Spencer weakens his case by an unnecessary adjective. The prejudice in favor one's own country is not senseless; and there are no more typical examples of claptrap than those which are only overemphatic appeals to patriotism.

The most ardent admirers of Sheridan as an orator cannot deny that he was often theatrical in his speechmaking; but they have the resource of pointing out that he was also patriotic in his playmaking. 'Pizarro' was the last piece to which he put his name; it was an effective adaptation of Kotzebue's 'Spaniards in Peru'; and it was originally brought out when England was endangered by the army which Napoleon had gathered at Boulogne. The famous address of Rolla to his fellow countrymen, adjuring them to unite in defence of their country against an invading foe, was only a reworking of a nobly patriotic speech which Sheridan himself had made only a little while before the play had its first performance; and when this eloquent harangue fell upon the ears of the audiences in Drury Lane, they could not but perceive the pertinence of Rolla's outburst to their own immediate situation. Perhaps this was claptrap, if we judge it harshly; yet it served a worthy purpose.

In this more sophisticated twentieth century patriotism for revenue only lingers belated in our light and lively musical pieces and in our kaleidoscopic reviews. In the British operettas the Gaiety girls keep step to tunes of tinkling triviality, 'Tommy Atkins' and 'Soldiers of the Queen'; and in the American summer-song-shows the more energetic chorus ladies wave the star-spangled banner and hail it as "a grand old rag!" The spectators in the theaters of London and New York, digesting their dinners and expecting nothing more than the idle amusement of an otherwise empty evening, may smile with tolerant superiority at the obviousness of this vocal and visual claptrap, dismissing it as a dead-set at their own sluggish patriotism; but, nevertheless, many of them feel a flutter of the pulse as the martial rhythms beat upon their ears and the banners dance before their eyes.

In the more serious drama and in the hands of a more skilful workman patriotic claptrap is sometimes artfully disguised as disparagement of the very people for whose pleasure the play has been written. Sardou, for example, in his 'Théodora,' attempted an authentic evocation of the decadent splendor of Byzantium. He was a trained investigator as well as an adroit playwright; and he utilized a heterogeny of curious customs to enrich the local color in which he had immersed his melodramatic story. To call the attention of his French audiences to the historical curiosities he had accumulated, he introduced a stranger, ignorant of Byzantine manners, a stranger for whose benefit the natives could elucidate whatever needed explanation. This wanderer from the heart of distant

133

Gaul, from a village on a little island in the Seine, he brought to the metropolis on the Bosporus, so that the Byzantines could smile at his ignorance and say to one another, "He's a Parisian, and, of course, he doesn't know anything about life and manners,"—an ironic flattery for the Parisian spectators of the play.

Sardou had earlier employed a similar device in 'Patrie,' his foremost historical drama, in which he dealt with episodes of the revolt of the Netherlands against the Spanish oppressor. He introduced a French nobleman, a gay and gallant young fellow, on a mission from his sovereign, a neutral therefore, but none the less a sympathetic spectator of the Belgian struggle, serving as a sort of Greek chorus to transmit to the audience the message of the author himself. Beneath the light-heartedness of this brave and buoyant Frenchman there is a capacity for deep feeling, disclosed only on occasion; and therefore he is a most attractive figure, subtly flattering to the pride of his fellow countrymen, sitting silent at a play.

No doubt, it would be unfair to dismiss as claptrap what Sardou did in these two dramas; and yet it is not easy to deny that this cleverest of playmakers was in fact setting "a trap to catch a clap by way of applause from the spectators at a play."

Those who inquire too curiously may, if they so choose, find in 'Hamlet' an anticipation of this ironic quip in 'Théodora.' And there is a certain external similarity between Sardou's Parisian visitor, who is necessarily ignorant of the things every Byzantine knew, and Shakspere's prince, who is feigning madness, and who will therefore excite no comment when he goes to England, since "there the men are as mad as he."

III

If those who inquire too curiously insist on pursuing their investigation in other plays than 'Hamlet,' they will find more than one instance of traps to catch applause from spectators by an overt appeal to the deep-seated love of the English for their ancestral island. Consider the long speech of John of Gaunt just before his death, in which he deplores the political situation in

> This royal throne of kings, this sceptered isle,
> This earth of majesty, this seat of Mars,
> This other Eden, demi-paradise,
> This fortress, built by Nature for herself,
> Against infection, and the hand of war;
> This happy breed of men, this little world,
> This precious stone set in the silver sea,

Which serves it in the office of a wall,
Or as a moat defensive to a house,
Against the envy of less happy lands;
This blessed plot, this earth, this realm, this Eng-
    land, . . .
This land of such dear souls, this dear, dear land,
Dear for her reputation throughout the world.

Taken by itself and apart from its context
the speech from which these lines have been
taken might be harshly dismissed as flagrant
claptrap; in fact, it has been held up to the
scorn of men with souls so dead that they have
never cared to listen to a word in favor of their
own country. But if any defence were needed
it could be based on two facts. The first is that
this lofty laudation is absolutely in character
and in situation; it is precisely what Gaunt felt
and thought at that special moment in that
special play. The second is that it has no taint
of insincerity. We cannot doubt that the poet
himself felt and thought what he made his character say. After all, Shakspere was an Englishman himself, a sturdy Elizabethan, having an
intimate sympathy with the sentiments and
emotions of his fellow Elizabethans, only recently released from the stress of the mighty
effort which beat back the Armada. The year
of the running sea-fight in the British Channel
is one of the years in Shakspere's life of which

we know nothing; and we may some day happen upon evidence in support of the daring suggestion that Shakspere himself served for a week or a month on one or another of the vessels of that mosquito fleet which manœuvred the stately ships of Spain to their dispersal and destruction.

No doubt, Euripides, born not long after the defeat of the Persians at Salamis, is as sincere in his eulogy of his own city as Shakspere was in his tribute to his own country; yet in his 'Medea' the Greek poet assigns to a chorus of the women of Colchis his pæan of praise to Athens, a lyric grateful to the ears of the audience in the Attic theater, but only doubtfully appropriate to the mouths of these dwellers in a distant town. In fact, a modern student of this ancient play can hardly help being struck by the obvious effort by which this beautiful ode is lugged in, so to speak. It scarcely seems to belong where the poet put it; and the suspicion is almost unavoidable that its presence in the 'Medea' may be due to the desire of the dramatist to curry favor with the Athenian judges who had the awarding of the prize.

No matter when or where it assembles, after all, an audience is an audience. Whether the spectators sat in the seats of the Theater of Dionysus or stood in the open yard of the Globe Theater, they were "sisters under their skins"

—in spite of their being nearly all of them men, both in Athens and in London. We know that the English groundlings and gallants whom Shakspere had to please were violent in their likings, and we are inclined to believe that the Greek dramatists had in mind a far more highly cultivated gathering; yet the shrewd Mahaffy was frank in asserting that the Athenians exhibited now and again "a great deficiency in that elegance and chastity of taste which they and their modern critics perpetually arrogate as their private property."

This quotation is taken from the Irish scholar's 'History of Greek Classical Literature'; and in his little monograph on Euripides (contributed to the series of 'Classical Writers') he was even more explicit. He remarked that there can be discovered in the plays of the author of 'Medea' more than one example of "an almost vulgar patriotism, which makes the national heroes paragons of perfection, the action of Athens the noble feature of the play, and the heroes of Sparta or of Thebes mean and disgusting. One whole play, the 'Andromache,' is devoted to blackening the characters of Hermione and Menelaus and of their country—a cheap highroad to popularity with an audience at bitter enmity and in deadly conflict with Sparta."

It is sad to note that once or twice Shakspere also trod this cheap highroad. In 'Henry V,' for instance, the French Dauphin is only a poor boaster in contrast with the valiant simplicity of the English King. In the same play the English are all brave and the French are frequently feeble fellows with little stomach for fighting; and this is an unfortunate misrepresentation, since it diminishes the value of the English victory at Agincourt. 'Henry V' is all Shakspere's; it bears his sign manual; but 'Henry VI' is probably due to a collaboration of two or three writers not yet ascertained. Therefore it is possible that Shakspere is not himself responsible for the degradation of the character of Jeanne Darc, a needlessly offensive defamation, closely resembling the unfair treatment of Hermione and Menelaus by Euripides.

IV

There is preserved in the "Table Talk" of Samuel Rogers an anecdote which the banker-poet was in the habit of telling. An Englishman and a Frenchman had to fight a duel; and it was arranged that they should be armed with pistols and shut in an unlighted room to fire at will. The Englishman, not desiring to kill his opponent, fired up the chimney—and brought down the Frenchman. Rogers used to add that whenever he told this story in France, he always put the Frenchman up the chimney.

(1920)

VIII

THE SCENE IS LAID

VIII

THE SCENE IS LAID

I

EVERY student of the stage is under obli-
gation to Sir Arthur Wing Pinero for the
distinction he has drawn between the strategy
and the tactics of the drama, strategy defining
the unchanging and eternal principles of playmaking, and tactics serving to describe the methods of performance, continually modified by
changing conditions in the theater and by the
many improvements in presentation due to the
advancing complexity of civilization. Strategy
imposes on the playwright the duty of arousing
the interest of the audience, of retaining it, of
increasing it as the action progresses, and finally
of satisfying it. Tactics are never permanent;
and in the past they have varied from century
to century and from country to country; where
Æschylus could delight the eyes of the Attic
audiences by the stately evolutions of the chorus,
Shakspere found his profit in alarms and excur-
sions, in witches and ghosts.

We are so accustomed to the tactics proper
in our theater to-day, that we have to make a

resolute effort to appreciate the propriety of the
tactics employed by the playwrights of long ago.
It is because the tactics of Shakspere differ as
widely from those of Molière as the tactics of
Ibsen differ from those of Euripides, that not a
few careless critics have failed to perceive that
all four of these great playwrights were unconsciously working in accord with the same principles of strategy. Euripides and Shakspere,
Molière and Ibsen, each in his own time, and
each in accord with the conditions of his own
theater and with the conventions which his own
audiences were in the habit of accepting, was
availing himself of the means at his command
to arouse, to retain, to increase and to satisfy
the interest of those who might come to see his
plays.

The strategy of the drama is necessarily the
same whether the work in hand is a tragedy or
a comedy, a melodrama or a farce. A good
play is a good play, whether it is an empty
artificiality or an authentic study of human
nature. A play may owe an ephemeral vogue
in the theater to its felicitous interpretation of
the mood of the moment, to its spectacular em-
bellishments, to the powerful personality of an
actor of compelling force, or even to the personal charm of a beautiful actress. But its
success will be insubstantial unless it is built

in accord with the unvarying principles of playmaking, with that strategy of the drama, which
is as unalterable as the laws of the Medes and
the Persians. Æschylus's Theater of Dionysus
is in ruins, the site of Shakspere's Globe Theater
is not known with absolute certainty, Molière's
Palais Royal Theater has long since been destroyed; yet the masterpieces which delighted
the spectators who flocked to these playhouses
in Athens, in London, and in Paris abide with
us to-day to testify to the fact that they were
constructed in accord with the unwritten rules
of dramaturgic strategy even if they also reveal
their compliance with the tactics which were
satisfactory to their several audiences.

II

MANY, if not most, of the differences in the
tactics employed in the theaters of different
times and of different countries have been due
to the modifications of the methods of indicat-
ing to the spectators the place or places where
the several episodes of the story are supposed
to take place.

The Athenian theater could have had little
or no scenery, as we now understand the term.
There was a long dressing-house in the rear of

the orchestra, serving as a background and having doors which might be used as the entrances to a palace or a temple. It is possible that there may have been placed in front of this a rock or two to indicate a mountain pass or a tree or two to indicate a grove. But if these ever were utilized, they were inadequate identification of the precise spot; and so we find the Attic dramatists carefully informing us in the first score or two of lines what the precise spot was, a dread defile in the Caucasus, the King's palace at Thebes, the residence of Medea at Corinth. Where the action begins, there it ends, at least in the immense majority of the Greek tragedies which have come down to us. Yet as this action, however massive it might be, had a story simple almost to the point of bareness, as we moderns may think, the dramatist had little difficulty in assembling his characters and in making them come together, one after another, in the appointed place.

The Elizabethan theater was also devoid of anything we should to-day call scenery. It had a bare stage, with a gallery at the back, the space beneath being shut off by the hanging curtains, which could be drawn aside or looped up to reveal any inner room that might be called for. Therefore, as there was no scenery to change, there could be no change of scene. It

146

used to be believed that the succession of places which we may discover in any one of Shakspere's was indicated by the display of placards identifying each of these places in turns. For this belief there is little warrant; and these placards would not have enlightened the illiterate groundlings who stood in the yard.

We must remember that the division of Shakspere's pieces into acts and scenes was not his doing; it was the work by his editors long after his death; and this division is most unfortunate, as it misrepresents his practice. Shakspere really laid his scene on the stage of the Globe Theater, on the unadorned platform which served as a neutral ground where any two characters might meet. Whenever he saw advantage in having his audience know what that neutral ground was to be at a given moment in his story, then he let one of the characters tell, if need be, frankly asking the name of the place, and perhaps describing it so that the spectators might visualize it for themselves as best they could. This Elizabethan practice, inherited from the medieval drama, made things easy for the playwright, because if the stage was a neutral ground which might be anywhere, any two characters could meet and talk and make love and quarrel without the spectators having any right to question the probability of their coming together at

147

any precise spot. It may seem to us a primitive method; but it was perfectly satisfactory to Shakspere's contemporaries; and he made it serve his purpose. It is one of the reasons, however, why it is so difficult to adjust his plays to our modern stage, where every locality is made manifest by its appropriate scenery.

Shakspere was more or less medieval in his methods; and Molière is the first of the moderns in that his theater was roofed and lighted and had scenery, sparse as this was. As he shared his stage with a company of Italian comedians, we find him in the majority of his plays utilizing the convenient set of the Comedy-of-Masks,— a public square with two houses on each side, in one or another of which the more important characters were supposed to reside. It was natural enough for the characters to happen upon one another in a public square; and if they chose to discuss their private affairs outdoors they were only conforming to what is more or less the custom in Italy to the present day. In Molière's loftier plays, in a social drama like 'Tartuffe' and in a high comedy like the 'Femmes Savantes,' the chief characters all belong to a single family; and it is therefore natural for them to meet in the main room of the family residence. Thus it is that Molière is able to comply with the alleged rule prescribing Unity

148

of Place—that is, that the scene of all the acts should be the same.

This rule continued to be enforced in France until the Romanticist Revolt of 1830; but it was never able to curb the more abundant energy of the dramatists of England, even in the eighteenth century, when English literature was most completely under the influence of the Classicists. Sheridan, writing toward the end of the century for a theater which had skilful scene-painters, did not hesitate to change the scene as often as he found convenient in the course of any one act. And his successors until after the middle of the nineteenth century profited by his example, never straining their invention to devise pretexts for bringing characters to a single obligatory place, and unhesitatingly shifting the scene to any other place where these characters might more naturally assemble and meet together.

III

APPARENTLY it was Lessing who, in his 'Minna von Barnhelm,' first made a compromise between the complexity of the English practice and the simplicity of the French. He adopted the method of making no change during an act, and of making any change he needed between

149

the acts. This had obvious advantages; and it is what we find in the dramas of Hugo and the elder Dumas as well as in the comedies of Scribe, Augier and the younger Dumas. In the middle years of the nineteenth century the dramatic literature of France set the model for the dramatic literatures of every other country. It was from Scribe, Augier and the younger Dumas that Ibsen learnt his trade; and in his social dramas he has only one scene to the act, —often going behind Lessing to Molière, and having only one scene for all his acts.

The single scene to the act was introduced into England by T. W. Robertson, who was followed in Great Britain by W. S. Gilbert, Henry Arthur Jones, Arthur Pinero, James M. Barrie and George Bernard Shaw, and in the United States by Bronson Howard, Augustus Thomas and Clyde Fitch. It was adopted in Germany by Sudermann and Hauptmann, in Italy by d'Annunzio, and in Spain by Echegaray and Benevente. It has so thoroly imposed itself on the drama of the twentieth century that playgoers are now a little surprised when they are expected to sit in darkness while the scene upon which the curtain has risen is changed for another scene upon which the curtain is to fall.

One reason why the method of one-set-to-the-act has won world-wide acceptance is that it enables the stage-director to achieve a more elaborate realism in his scenery, furniture, and accessories. To-day we are accustomed to see characters living, moving and having their being in surroundings not only appropriate but characteristic. Neither playwright nor playgoer is satisfied if the drawing-room is merely a drawing-room; they want it to suggest the drawing-room of the heroine of that particular play, frankly characteristic of her and subtly expressing her personality. If the stage is supposed to represent the library of a gentleman and a scholar, we expect it to have that appearance, more or less exactly; and if it is shown to us as the dining-room of a vulgar profiteer, we are pleased to observe the obvious evidences of his pretentiousness. Playwrights and producers have been scrupulous in creating for playgoers this atmospheric harmony; and we have now become so exacting in our demands for it that it would not be easy to get us to accept the more or less makeshift furnishings which were considered adequate threescore years ago when it was the custom to shift the scenes three or four times in the course of an act.

During the past half-century the single-set-to-the-act has been found to have many advantages; and there is little likelihood that there will be a permanent return to any of the earlier methods, the frequent scene-shifting during the acts or the sceneless stage of the Tudor theater. It is true that there are abundant signs of a revolt against the mangling and mutilation which our modern scenic complexity has imposed upon the revivals of Shakspere's comedies and tragedies. Various efforts have been made to recover at least a little of the large freedom of the Elizabethan platform and to combine as far as may be possible the beauty of modern decoration with a simplicity more in accord with Shakspere's own methods.

While the single-set-to-the-act is perfectly acceptable for modern plays, constructed to meet its conditions, it is far less satisfactory when it compels readjustments of tragedies which were composed in compliance with conditions entirely dissimilar. And even if no one of the efforts in this direction can be called completely successful, they serve to indicate the path along which progress is possible. The sumptuous spectacular adornment which might be given to the 'Midsummer Night's Dream' or to 'Tempest' is not demanded by the severer stories of 'Hamlet' and 'Othello.' Of late we have seen welcome modifications of the method of charms of which Henry Irving availed himself with skill and taste and liberality, in favor of a presentation less sumptuous but not less beautiful in its comparative simplicity and not achieved at the sacrifice of Shakspere's own construction of his story.

IV

For most of the plays of to-day, comedies and social dramas, farces and even melodramas, the single-set-to-the-act has many advantages; yet it has also certain disadvantages. For one thing, it puts a severe strain upon the ingenuity of the playwright in that it compels him to invent a satisfactory explanation for the arrival of each of the characters, one after another, into the same room. These characters may belong to different stations in life; they may be almost unknown to one another; they may even have reason of their own for avoiding one another; yet they must be brought together in the place which the playwright has chosen as the scene of his act. What is more, their appearance in the play must seem to be the result of their own volitions. As each of them walks on the stage the spectators must be made to perceive at once, and with as little explanation as possible, the motive which has brought him. And this motive must be not only instantly apparent but obviously plausible. If the motive does not seem adequate, our attention is thereby

153

distracted more or less; and the playwright has failed to conserve what Herbert Spencer called the Economy of Attention.

This is a difficult feat to accomplish; and that it is achieved in the majority of modern plays is testimony to the technical dexterity of the dramatists of to-day, a dexterity far exceeding that demanded of the dramatists of yesterday. Shakspere did not have to solve this problem, since his sceneless platform was a neutral ground which might be anywhere and on which any two of his characters could meet without cavil; and Sheridan, in his turn, had not to wrestle with this difficulty, since he could change his scene at will, and if his characters did not want to meet at the appointed place, all he had to do was to change the place to one where they would come together willingly.

The easiest way for the playwright to get his characters together is to choose for their reunion a place and a moment when the spectators would expect a variety of persons to assemble. This is one of the explanations why the modern dramatist is forever inviting us to dinner or to afternoon tea or to a ball, all of these occasions when groups are collected. But here he has to surmount another stumbling-block; he must find satisfactory reasons for temporarily getting rid of the rest of those present so that the hero and heroine can have their intimate discussion of their private affairs; and this is a task quite as delicate; altho it may be a little less difficult, because the spectator will presumably be eager to listen to the lovers, and therefore he will be tolerant of the excuses which result in their being left alone for as long as may be necessary.

In view of this second difficulty the playwright may prefer to a place where people assemble, a drawing-room or an Italian garden, a place where people are only passing through, the office of a hotel or a room in a museum. The hotel office is especially useful for a first act in which an unrelated host of characters may be introduced without in any way departing from the facts of every-day experience. Mr. George M. Cohan utilized a country hotel in the opening act of 'Get-Rich-Quick Wallingford,' an act which was a masterpiece of exposition; and Mr. William de Mille used a city hotel in the opening act of the 'Woman' with corresponding felicity of effect. The room in the Vatican Museum which contains the statue of the Apollo Belvedere was selected by Clyde Fitch as the scene of one act in the 'Girl with the Green Eyes.'

Here Clyde Fitch was revolting against the monotonously stereotyped succession of afternoon teas, garden-parties, studio receptions, and other occasions for free and easy assembly. He was deliberately seeking to be different and to grace his play with a novel and attractive set. In this pursuit of the unexpected he put one act of the 'Stubbornness of Geraldine' on the deck of an ocean steamer, and one act of 'Her Great Match' in the fortune-teller's tent of a charity bazaar, thereby gaining the privilege of presenting his heroine in a picturesque gipsy costume. In a third play, the 'Climbers,' he sent a runaway couple to a little French restaurant overhanging the Bronx, where they were tracked by other persons in the story.

Mr. Augustus Thomas took as the scene for one act of the 'Other Girl' the back-yard of a New York dwelling, arranged as an outdoor summer resting-place; and Sir Arthur Pinero took as the scene of one act of his 'Letty' the roof of a London house, also made more or less comfortable for warm weather. In another of Pinero's plays, the 'Gay Lord Quex,' one act passes in the main room of a manicure's establishment; and in Mr. Shaw's 'You Never Can Tell,' one act passes in the office of a dentist. And Mr. Henry Arthur Jones, not to be outdone, took the leading characters of his 'Masqueraders' to the astronomical observatory at Nice.

V

WHETHER the modern dramatist has to avail himself of the drawing-room while there is dancing in the next room, or whether he is at liberty to select a less shop-worn spot because he needs to bring together only two or three characters, he must always conceive each of his acts, whatever its scene, as a unit, as one of the three or four units which combine to make his play. He plans his plot as a whole and he plans each of its acts as an integral part of this whole. Each act must be complete in itself, and yet proportioned absolutely to the rest of the play. His acts are the blocks with which he builds his towering column, the first act being its base and the last act its capital. Where Shakspere thought of his play as an uninterrupted story, to be shown in action on the stage, with only such intermissions as might be for the convenience of the audience, the modern dramatist has to think in terms of separate acts, each of them adjusted to the place wherein its action is to pass. Before he begins to write the dialog of any act, he has to visualize the set and to see in his mind's eye the movements of his characters in the scenery he has designed for them.

Now, this is a new departure in dramatic art.

It is something which does not antedate Lessing. It is something which was first turned to account by the adroit French dramatists of the middle of the nineteenth century. It is something which the dramatists of every other country have gladly taken over from the French. It is something which the French dramatists of the late sixteenth century knew nothing about. In his invaluable outline for a history of French dramatic literature, M. Gustave Lanson made it clear that the founders of French tragedy, Jodelle for one, and Garnier for another, brought on the stage the characters they needed, not designating any precise locality but leaving it doubtful, "perhaps without even giving it a thought." And what Jodelle and Garnier were doing in France is almost exactly what Marlowe and Kyd were doing in England in those same years For reasons of his own Molière departed from the practice of Jodelle and Garnier, while Shakspere, also for reasons of his own, conformed to that of Kyd and Marlowe.

(1920)

IX

THE DEVELOPMENT OF SCENIC DEVICES

IX

THE DEVELOPMENT OF SCENIC DEVICES

I

IT is not far from forty years since I paid my first visit to the dramatic museum of the Paris Opéra, then newly housed in the left wing of the sumptuous edifice,—the wing originally designed to provide a private entrance for Napoleon III. There, in a narrow passageway, were models of a dozen of the most striking sets which had been painted for the masterpieces of the music-drama in the preceding half-century; and there, in a broad and spacious gallery, were models of stage-machinery, sketches for costumes, playbills, ancient and modern, autograph letters of famous composers, and original manuscript scores of a few of the long sequence of famous operas written specially for the French National Academy of Music. The founder of the museum of the Opéra was Charles Nuitter; and he was kind enough to serve as my guide and to call my attention to the most interesting exhibits.

As was natural, we fell into talk about the

history of scene-painting and about the modern elaboration of scenic effect and mechanical device; and in the course of our conversation Nuitter sent for a tall and stately tome full of engraved illustrations.

"We are inclined to pride ourselves," he said to me, "on our modern improvements; and most of us are likely to believe that our predecessors of the last century could not compete with us in the ingenuity and in the complexity of the effects we can now produce on the stage. But if you will examine this book, Sabbatini's 'Art of Making Scenery and Theatrical Machines,' published in Italian in 1638 at Ravenna, you will discover that there has been little advance in the past two and a half centuries. Those Italians could do then almost everything that we can do now on the stage of the Opéra. For example, look at this plate, and you will see that they were prepared to exhibit a full-rigged ship, to bring it on under sail, and to make it manœuver in front of the spectators. We could scarcely do it any better nowadays; and we should have to do it very much in the same way. In one thing, and in one thing only, have we an indisputable advantage over the Italian painter-engineers whose inventiveness has been commemorated by Sabbatini. We have artificial light and an abundance of it,

while they were dependent either upon daylight
or upon the wholly inadequate illumination of
sputtering candles and of smoking oil-lamps."

In this last remark Nuitter pointed out the
essential difference between the modern theater
since Molière's time and all earlier theaters,
those in ancient Greece and Rome and those in
Renascence Italy, in the England of Elizabeth
and in the Spain of Philip. All these earlier
playhouses had to give their performances by
daylight; and most of their spectators were exposed to the sun and the rain. And even in
Molière's time, and in fact until the introduction of gas early in the nineteenth century, the
lighting of the stage was pitiably insufficient.
In fact, we might go further and maintain that
there was no wholly satisfactory means of theatrical illumination until the invention of the
electric light toward the end of the nineteenth
century, altho the introduction of the calcium
light a few years earlier had made possible not
a few effects unattainable by gas alone.

When we consider the extraordinary variety
and the subtle delicacy of the methods of apply-
ing the electric light, as these have been developed in the first quarter of the twentieth
century, we are inclined to doubt whether the
stage-managers of a century ago, of three centuries ago and of twenty centuries ago could

163

have achieved anything fairly entitled to be called spectacle, as we now use the word. But the audiences of those distant days were unable to foresee our modern appliances; they could not miss what they did not know; and they were delighted by devices which were perfectly satisfactory to them, even if they would strike us to-day as painfully primitive and absurdly inadequate. Indeed, it is interesting to discover that they often attempted in their unroofed playhouses effects not unlike those to which we are accustomed in our well-lighted theaters.

There is the so-called Flying Ballet, for example, in which dancers, suspended by invisible wires, float ethereally across the stage almost as tho they were birds or butterflies. Yet the Greeks more than twenty centuries ago had a simpler device, not exactly equivalent to this but not altogether unlike it. When one of their adroit dramatists desired to have a God descend from the sky, he made use of what was then known as the "machine." Apparently this was nothing more than a basket, appropriately decorated to look like a chariot, which was hoisted by a rope over a pulley and then lowered to allow the unexpected deity to step down among the other actors standing in the orchestra.

Another Greek anticipation of a modern effect is the "ekkeklema," which brought before the

eyes of the enthralled spectators something supposed to have taken place out of sight. In the
'Agamemnon' of Æschylus, Clytemnestra goes
into her palace to murder her husband with the
aid of her paramour, Ægisthus. After an interval of dread anticipation the audience heard the
cry of the murdered man; and then the wide
central doors of the palace were thrown open
and a little platform on wheels was thrust forward on which the spectators could behold the
corpse of Agamemnon with his assassin wife
standing over him. This is not unlike the vision
of Margaret, evoked by Mephistopheles to tempt
Faust to his perdition. Where the Greeks had
to roll into view a "living picture," so to speak,
the modern stage-manager suddenly makes a
portion of the back-scene transparent, slightly
darkening the stage and focussing a very strong
light upon the innocent heroine spinning at her
wheel and singing as she spins.

The later Latins allowed their noble theaters to be given over to variety shows, to
pantomimists, to acrobats, and rope-dancers. In
Rome the true drama had succumbed to the
bitter rivalry of the gladiatorial combat, which
evoked a swifter and more poignant ecstasy
than any play, however powerful, could be expected to provide. The drama was unable to
compete with this grosser presentation of a life-

and-death struggle. The spectacles to be seen in the Roman Colosseum were as sumptuous as they were varied. Sometimes the huge arena was filled with a transplanted forest, and wild animals were let loose to roam amid the trees, awaiting the arrows of the expert archers whose duty it was to slay them at the risk of their own lives. On other occasions this same vast space was flooded with water; and fleets of galleys manned by gladiators and rowed by slaves took part in naval battles fought out to the death of a majority of the combatants.

II

WHEN the passion-play was elaborated in the churches of the Middle Ages, the learned priests bestowed upon it all the spectacle possible with their resources. They had singing and costumes and processions; they guided the Three Kings who were carrying splendid gifts to the Holy Babe in the Manger, by a lamp pulled along a wire over their heads to suggest the Star of Bethlehem. And in the course of the years, after the passion-play had developed into the mystery-play and after it had been thrust out of the church to be acted by devout laymen in the market-place, a heterogeny of ingenious devices was employed to arrest and retain the attention

166

of immense crowds which collected from the surrounding country to gaze on the representation of the successive episodes of the Bible story. In the Garden of Eden the Tree of Life was encircled by a mechanical serpent, which twined itself around the trunk, raising its glittering head and projecting its forked tongue. The Mouth of Hell was generally represented by the jaws of a great dragon breathing fierce flames upon the evil-doer as the nimble devils cast him into the fiery opening. A little later yet, when the lives of the saints were dramatized, the several martyrdoms of these holy men were represented with the utmost elaboration of realism, Saint Sebastian being transfixt by a flight of arrows and Saint Lawrence being roasted on a red-hot gridiron.

In the Italian Renascence, mythological stories were occasionally performed with all possible pomp and splendor in the beautiful grounds of the princely villas. In the Dramatic Museum of Columbia University there is a large engraving of the gardens of the Pitti Palace in Florence at the moment when a towering statue of Atlas, bearing the world on his back, has been drawn to the center of the arena, so that the globe can open and disgorge certain of the characters of the story. These ornate spectacles of the Italians, elaborated by the aid of the leading

167

painters, were generally given outdoors, altho now and again we hear of one which was produced in the ballroom of a palace, illuminated for the occasion by thousands of wax candles. Here in these magnificent productions of the Renascence Italians we may find the parent of the court-ballet of the French and of the masque of the English; and here we may find also (if we insist upon it) the grandparent of the sumptuously decorated music-drama as of our own day, of which Wagner's 'Parsifal' is perhaps the most notable example.

Complaint was made, and with justice, that in the last years of the last century managers overdecorated their revivals of Shakspere's plays, sometimes even obscuring the dramatic force of a tragedy in certain of its episodes by the distracting trappings with which the plays were encumbered. Yet if we study the whole series of Shakspere's comedies and tragedies and histories, we cannot escape the conclusion that he had no dislike for decoration, and that he was swift to seize every opportunity to provide spectacle. To a twentieth-century producer the resources of Shakspere's playhouse would seem to be sorely restricted; but, such as they were, Shakspere availed himself of them to the utmost. He was lavish with duels and battles and sieges, set off with trumpet-calls and cannon-shots; and he was liberal with processions and with trials in court. In 'Lear' he had three terrific storms in swift succession; and in the 'Tempest' he had half-a-dozen magical transformations not unlike those we associate with the old-fashioned fairy-play.

In the Elizabethan theater the stage was roofed and so were the galleries which ran around the other three sides; but the yard was open to the sky, exposing the groundlings to the frequent rain and letting in all the light necessary for the performance. How was it then that the stage-manager was able to suggest the darkness of night in Juliet's garden and in Macbeth's castle? This question has been the cause of a plentiful waste of ink on the part of those commentators who fail to understand the simplicity of the Elizabethan playhouse and to appreciate the childlike willingness of Elizabethan audiences to "make believe." We have even been told that the windows of the theater were darkened whenever the scene was supposed to take place at night; and this grotesque suggestion is characteristic of the crass absurdity of a great deal of Shaksperian criticism. When the stage was flooded with the effulgence of a westering sun, curtains hung before the windows would produce no sensible diminution of the light; and when the eyes of the spectators were focused on

169

the stage they would not perceive the obscuring of the openings in the walls behind them. The valid explanation is very simple; the audience accepted the word of the dramatist; and if he asserted that the stage was shrouded in midnight blackness, they never cavilled, just as they were satisfied when "three back-swords eked a battle out" or when a "rolled bullet" served to suggest the deep grumbling of thunder.

It is an interesting matter for speculation what Shakspere would think if he could visit this changed world of ours and see for himself the many alterations in the methods of the theater. As he was a modest man, he would be astonished at the immensity of his reputation, and as he was a man with an abiding sense of humor, he would glance at the lucubrations of his commentators with a disrespectful smile. But in the playhouse itself he would find himself at home; and it may be doubted whether he would feel any impulse to protest against the lavishness with which his plays have been mounted. He would see instantly that this lavishness increased the attractiveness of his plays to the main body of the playgoing public; —and it was to this main body of the playgoing public that he had always addressed himself. He had a keen eye to the main chance; he was a thrifty person with money out at interest;

and he would understand easily and appreciate readily the changed conditions of theatrical performance. Probably nothing would astonish him more or seem to him more inexplicable than the electric light, available anywhere and anywhen; and possibly he would be frank in expressing his regret that he had been denied the privilege of using it.

III

THE electric light is a late nineteenth-century improvement in the playhouse; and Shakspere, altho he is for all time and therefore on occasion surprisingly modern in his utterances, was not and could not be modern in his methods, since his bare stage had a host of resemblances to the platform of the players of mysteries and moralities in the Middle Ages. Molière is really the earliest of the moderns; and, altho Calderon actually survived Molière, the Spanish theater for which he composed his lyric melodramas was quite as medieval in its methods as the English theater in Shakspere's day. And even if Molière is indisputably a modern, he is only the earliest of the moderns. He wrote for a playhouse which was roofed and for a stage dimly illuminated by a pair of chandeliers containing a dozen candles each,—chandeliers that hung over the

171

edge of the stage and that had to be lowered at intervals during the performance so that the candles might be snuffed.

Molière's playhouse might be roofed and his stage might be lighted, more or less; but otherwise this stage was almost as bare as Shakspere's; and like Shakspere's it was cluttered at the sides by seats for the men about town, whose presence sadly restricted the area available for the actors. All the acting had to be done well down in front, beneath the chandeliers and between the seated spectators on the right and left of the stage, so there was no room for any furniture, for tables or chairs or sofas. In Molière's plays, as in Shakspere's, all the characters had to stand all the time;—that is to say, nobody ever sat down, unless the action of the play absolutely demanded it. On these rare occasions, it is probable that the needed furniture was brought on just before it had to be used.

The intruding and obtruding spectators usurped a large share of the stage in the Théâtre Français for more than a hundred years after Molière's death, whereas the English stage got rid of them a little earlier. Very possibly it was, in some measure, due to this disincumbering of the stage that English tragedy was more spectacular than French, and that it more often called in the aid of the scene-painter and of the stage-carpenter. At any rate, there seems to be pretty good reason for believing that "grooves" to sustain "wings" and "flats" were first used by Inigo Jones; and that their use spread from England to the Continent. There were from three to five sets of these grooves, depending on the depth of the stage; they were all masked above by "borders"; and they were all available either for "wings" or "flats." When the flats were run on in the grooves nearest to the footlights, the scene was said to be "set in one," and when it was said to be "set in five" the four other grooves were used to support four pairs of wings. If the scene was outdoors, then the wings were "tree wings" and the borders were "sky borders," strips of cloth painted a light blue.

Since the invention of the "box-set" (about the middle of the nineteenth century) "grooves" survive only in the vaudeville houses and in the toy-theaters which delighted us in our childhood. It was an advantage of the earlier system of sliding flats, now in "one" and now in "three," that the playwright could shift his scene as often as he saw fit, perhaps even half-a-dozen times in the course of a single act; but it was a disadvantage that an interior, a library, for example, had no walls or windows or doors, except such as might be painted on the wings, ranged one behind the other parallel with the footlights and permitting the characters to enter at any "entrance" (as the space between the wings was called). To those who were used to this convention, there was nothing incongruous in this walking on of the persons of the play through the walls, or at least through where the walls ought to have been.

The "box-set," now familiar to us all, enables us to have a room with its walls and its ceiling, its doors and its windows, its furniture, its pictures and its hangings. It differs from a real room in a real house only in the absence of the fourth wall, which if present would prevent the spectators from seeing the stage. It was probably first employed in France, but it was so obvious and so necessary an improvement that it was speedily transplanted to England. It may be only a coincidence, but there seems to be significance in the fact that the box-set was not devised until after the introduction of gas made it possible to light the theater satisfactorily. The English stage had had footlights in the seventeenth century, when they were probably candles with tin reflectors behind them. In the eighteenth century oil-lamps had been substituted for candles; and in many theaters these lamps were fastened to a long board which was called the "float" and which could be lowered

174

beneath the stage during the intermissions so
that the wicks might be trimmed. And now in
the twentieth century there is a movement to
do away with the footlights, which necessarily
illumine the faces of the actors from below,
whereas light naturally comes from above. By
the aid of "spot-lights" and of "baby-spots"
it is possible to provide an illumination which
does not come from one direction only, but which
is more or less diffused, as the sunlight is. As a
result the stage looks less stagy.

There is no denying that the latter-day dramatist is far less devoted to mechanical devices
than his predecessors were in the middle of the
last century. His interest is now centered in
what his characters are, in what they feel and in
what they think, rather than in what they do. In
other words, the drama is moving away from
melodrama, which it is abandoning to the
"movies." Sensational scenes, such as gripped
our grandfathers sixty years ago, have been
banished from the better sort of theater; they
seem to us too violent, too artificial and too
obviously mechanical. The device of the rising
tower in 'Arrah-na-Pogue,' and the kindred device of the turning-tower in the 'Shaughraun,'
would seem to most of us to-day more or less
out of place in the playhouse and at home only
in the "moving-picture palace." Perhaps, if

the inventor of these two spectacular effects, Dion Boucicault, were alive to-day he might be composing clever comedies closely modeled on the realities of life and wholly without any surplusage of mechanical effect, or (what is perhaps more probable) he might be making a fortune as the director of a moving-picture studio, where his gift of invention, and his still larger faculty of adaptation, would be most profitably employed.

(1917)

X

MEMORIES OF ACTRESSES

X

MEMORIES OF ACTRESSES

I

ACTORS have always held it as their peculiar misfortune that their work perishes with them and that they can leave behind them only the reputation they achieved in the practice of their profession—a reputation unsupported by tangible evidence. Moreover, even when the judgment of their own generation has been favorable, it is likely soon to fade away because it has nothing to validate it except the unsubstantial echo of departed popularity. Joseph Jefferson used to say sadly that the actor could survive solely in the written record of the impression he made upon his contemporaries. That is to say, he can continue to exist only by virtue of their record of his achievement—his work having ceased to be at the very moment it came into being. If this commemoration shall fail him, then the abundant and superabundant applause he may have fed upon while he was on the stage will avail nothing to preserve him from swift oblivion. The fiery ardor of Edmund Kean still burns brightly in the luminous pages of Hazlitt and of Lewes; and the incomparable versatility of Coquelin is still made manifest for us in the essays of Francisque Sarcey and of Henry James.

Altho I yield myself willingly to the contagious enthusiasm of Hazlitt and Lewes, Sarcey and James, I lack their power of recapturing their emotions and I have not their art of delicate discrimination. None the less do I feel that I should be ungrateful for past delights if I shrank from setting down a few of the most outstanding of my countless histrionic reminiscences. For sixty years now I have been an incessant and indefatigable playgoer. In my attempt at an autobiography, 'These Many Years,' and in one or another of my volumes of essays on the theater, I have tried to assemble and to classify my recollections of the more important of the actors I have known, on the stage and off, Booth and Irving, Coquelin and Salvini, John T. Raymond and Nat Goodwin; and now I am moved to recall and set in order my reminiscences of certain actresses, who smile back at me as I hold up before them the mirror of memory.

When I had the youthful privilege of beholding Charlotte Cushman, Adelaide Ristori, and Adelaide Neilson, I was too immature in judgment and too ignorant of the art of acting to form opinions worthy of record; but none the less do I cherish the immediate impression, even if I can do no more now than testify to the austere power of Miss Cushman as Queen Katherine, to the dignity and pathos of Signora Ristori as Marie Antoinette, and to the fragile charm of Miss Neilson as Juliet. I thrill again as I recall dimly the startling appearance of Charlotte Cushman as Meg Merrilies and the sinister suggestion which Ristori as Lucrezia Borgia insinuated into her "Don Alphonso d'Este, my *third* husband!" Unfortunately, my recollections of these actresses seen only twice or thrice in my boyhood are too few and too faint for me to revive them now after half-a-century; and I must perforce draw upon later recollections abiding with me more solidly because I was older and better prepared to appreciate and because I had more frequent occasion to accumulate impressions.

II

Ristori was an Italian who acted in French in Paris and in English in New York, and who conquered her audiences in France and in America in spite of her alien accents. Fechter was a Frenchman who had spoken English from his youth up but who was never able to acquire the rhythm of our sharply accented tongue. Modjeska was a Pole who learned English only when she was a mature woman; and her speech always revealed itself as foreign, altho some of her ardent admirers accepted this exotic flavor as adding piquancy to her delivery. That an Italian, a Frenchman and a Pole established themselves on the American stage, despite their incomplete mastery of English, may testify to our cosmopolitan hospitality, but it is evidence also of the artistic accomplishment of these polyglot immigrants.

I saw Modjeska during her first engagement in New York when she was appearing in well-worn plays of an approved popularity, the 'Lady of the Camellias' and 'Adrienne Lecouvreur.' She had no difficulty in transmitting the customary emotion of the death-scenes of these unfortunate heroines. She had the gift of compelling tears; she had power and reserve; she could be brilliant without being metallic. What I recall in her performance of that lachrimatory consumptive Camille was her standing by the fireplace in the first act, toasting a dainty slipper and telling her lover "You see, I am very expensive"—a firm and delicate stroke. And I saw her later when she took possession of a series of Shakspere's heroines, always dangerous for one not native to our speech; and of all these impersonations I found Rosalind the most satisfactory in its archness, its womanliness, its coquetry.

She was a consummate artist, with absolute command of all her resources; yet she did not achieve the essential Englishry of Rosalind. She remained continental and not insular. As my friend H. C. Bunner put it aptly, "Modjeska's Rosalind would be perfect—if only we could admit that Rosalind is a pretty French widow." It was exquisite; it had high breeding and playful wit; it had every excellence—but it was exotic; and perhaps it was a little too complicated, a little too lacking in the simplicity which is an undeniable quality of Shakspere's English girl. At times Modjeska's art was perilously close to artificiality. I do not mean to imply that she was ever stagy or theatrical; she was too completely a mistress of her craft for any overstress of this sort; but she could not quite attain to that concealment of her art which is the ultimate perfection of craftsmanship. It was shrewdly said of Duse that "she sometimes overacted her underacting"; and it can be said of Modjeska that she never felt any temptation to underact. She gave good measure, pressed down, yet not running over.

It was this slight suggestion of artifice which sharpened an anecdote (perhaps apocryphal). Maurice Barrymore was her leading man for several seasons and he was the author of a boldly effective piece, 'Nadjesda,' which she had included in her repertory but which she did not put in the bill as often as he desired and expected. When he urged her to appear in his piece more frequently, she explained that she found the part of Nadjesda very fatiguing, in fact, almost exhausting. Whereupon Barry blurted out, "You would have more strength to act at night, Madame, if you didn't act so much in the daytime!"

Shocked by this unexpected attack, she accused him of ingratitude.

"And why should I be grateful to you?" asked Barry.

"I have done so much for you," Modjeska explained. "I have taken you with me all over the United States. I have made you known."

"Made me known?" he returned indignantly, for he also had his full portion of the artistic temperament. "Let me tell you, Madame, that Maurice Barrymore was known from Portland, Maine, to Portland, Oregon, when nobody knew whether Modjeska was a tooth-wash or what!"

III

I DOUBT if I ever saw two actresses more divergent in their personalities and in their methods than Modjeska and Clara Morris. One was the fine flower of European culture, and the other a wilding bloom of our own virgin soil, vigorous and uncultivated. Modjeska spoke English with an alien intonation; and Clara Morris had an accent of her own, which Londoners would have considered "American" and which New Yorkers called "Western." Modjeska had studied her art in a community with rich esthetic traditions, under competent guidance, whereby she developed taste and discretion; and Clara Morris had spent the years of her youth in the stock company of an inland city where the bill was changed weekly and sometimes nightly. She began as an extra in the ballet; she was later intrusted with "utility parts"; and as she gained experience she rose to characters as important as Emilia in 'Othello.' Her schooling was arduous, varied and invaluable; but it was deficient in imparting the delicate refinements of the art of acting. If only she could have had the severe training of a conservatory she would have been one of the foremost actresses of America. Even as it was she made an outstanding place for herself.

It was to the Othello of E. L. Davenport, one of the most vigorous and versatile actors of half-a-century ago, that she played Emilia; and when Davenport joined the stock company with

which Augustin Daly opened the Fifth Avenue
Theater, he recommended her. Daly engaged
her, to play any part he might assign; and her
chance came when Agnes Ethel, the favorite
pupil of Matilda Heron, found herself too fa-
tigued (after the long run of 'Froufrou') to
undertake the heroine of a dramatization of
'Man and Wife.' In her autobiography, not deficient in self-appreciation, she does not over-
state the extent of her unexpected success as
Anne Sylvester. With that part she established
herself in the good opinion of the New York
playgoers, who recognized the power and the
sincerity of the performance, even if they were
also acutely conscious of her occasional crudity.
Despite this exhibition of her skill, Daly, who
was the most autocratic of managers, cast her
the next season as one of the half-dozen girls
who existed merely to be recipients of the inter-
mittent attentions of the imperfectly monogamous hero of Bronson Howard's 'Saratoga.'

Her chance came again when Daly adapted
a turgid and tawdry melodrama, 'Article 47,'
by Adolphe Bélot, and cast Clara Morris as
Cora. I recall the absorbed stillness during the
final act at the first performance of this play,
when Cora was seated on one side, taking no
part in the dialog, and when we suddenly became
aware, I know not by what means, that the

silent woman rocking her body to and fro was going mad before our eyes. That was Clara Morris's hour of triumph; and there was no doubt that she deserved it. Her acting might be unequal and uncertain; but now and again it was illumined by flashes of insight and inspiration; and in 'Article 47' she displayed histrionic imagination. So she did a little later in 'Alixe,' a lachrymose heroine, whom she impersonated with touching pathos. I recall this performance in 'Alixe' as the perfection of simplicity in accord with the poignancy of the situation.

After she left Daly's, she went to the Union Square, where she had a part entirely within her compass, the weepful heroine of a weepful play, 'Miss Multon,' an adroit rehandling of the story of 'East Lynne' by two skilful Parisian playwrights, Nus and Bélot. Clara Morris had not only the power of compelling tears from the spectators, she could herself shed them at will. That admirable comedian, James Lewis, who was with her in the company at Daly's as he had been with her in her 'prentice days at Cleveland, used to say to her, "Cry for us, Clara, won't you?"—and the obedient tears would course down her cheek. The gift of tears is not uncommon, but it is rarely possessed by the most accomplished actresses; and therefore it is sometimes despised by those who hold that the art of acting must be always independent of the emotion of the moment. Coquelin, the best equipt of comedians, once said to me that a certain actress of great popularity "actually weeps on the stage—therefore she is a mediocre artist." Highly as I rated Coquelin's opinions about the art in which he excelled, I confess that this seemed to me a harsh judgment. No doubt, Coquelin agreed with the remark that Emile Augier is reported to have uttered to a temperamental actor rehearsing a leading part, —"A little less genius, if you please, and a little more talent!"

The last time I saw Clara Morris was when she headed the English-speaking company engaged to support Salvini, and when she played the wife of Conrad in the 'Morte Civile.' I can pay her performance of this pathetic part no higher compliment than to express my opinion that she was not unworthy to stand by the side of the Italian tragedian. She had dignity and reserve; she curbed her old-time exuberance, and she displayed all her old-time power. She controlled her genius and exhibited her talent. In her account of her career she took pleasure in telling us that she was able to suggest to Salvini a modification of a customary piece of "business," a suggestion which he accepted as an improvement. She had a gift of invention; and she earlier recorded a novel effect devised by her when she was acting Emilia to the Othello of E. L. Davenport.

There was a delicate discrimination in the complimentary lines which Edmund Clarence Stedman sent to Clara Morris when once she reappeared on the New York stage after a prolonged absence:

> Touched by the fervor of her art,
>   No flaws to-night discover!
> Her judge shall be the people's heart,
>   This Western world her lover.
> The secret given to her alone
>   No frigid schoolman taught her:—
> Once more returning, dearer grown,
>   We greet thee, Passion's daughter.

IV

At one time or another Augustin Daly managed four theaters in New York. Clara Morris appeared in 'Man and Wife' at the original Fifth Avenue Theater in 24th Street. When this was destroyed by fire, Daly opened a house in Broadway opposite Waverly Place, which had been a church and which was later the Old London Street; and it was there that Clara Morris played in 'Alixe.' Then the second

189

Fifth Avenue Theater (still standing on the corner of Broadway and 28th Street) was built for Daly; and there Clara Morris acted in 'Article 47.' After several unprofitable seasons Daly was forced to relinquish management, but after an interval he was able to secure control of Wood's Museum on the corner of Broadway and 30th Street, remodeling it and calling it Daly's Theater. This house was under his direction until his death; and it was there that Ada Rehan slowly won her way into the affections of our playgoers.

I recall distinctly the impression she made upon me on the opening night. She played an inconspicuous part in 'Newport,' Olive Logan's clumsy perversion of 'Niniche.' She was then a lank and gawky girl, and in one scene she had to wear an unbecoming bathing-suit. The play did not please; and the newcomer did not attract any attention. No one could then foresee that, under the judicious guidance of Daly, she would develop into a performer capable of carrying off the leading parts in Shakspere's comedies. Only by degrees did she advance in her art and capture the admiration of the public. With John Drew as her partner, with James Lewis and Mrs. G. H. Gilbert to complete the quartet, she frolicked and rollicked through a swift succession of Daly's arbitrary localizations of pieces by the German playwrights. In these she disclosed an American sense of fun and a Celtic exuberance of humor; and her singing of 'Miss Jenny O'Jones' was an exhilarating exhibition of comic force; of sheer comic force, of spontaneous and effervescent gaiety.

In time these contemporary farces alternated with older and old-fashioned comedies which forced her to broaden her methods and to refine her style. Perhaps she was most abundantly successful as Peggy Thrift in Garrick's 'Country Girl' (a most skilful deodorization of Wycherley's unspeakable 'Country Wife'). But only second to this were her successive impersonations of the heroines of 'She Would and She Would Not,' the 'Recruiting Officer' and the 'Inconstant.' As she gained in experience, her figure filled out and her beauty made itself manifest. She had a wholesome femininity; and her winning personality never appeared to better advantage than when the heroines she impersonated had to disguise themselves in manly attire—a useful preparation for her later appearances as Rosalind, Viola, and Portia. Year by year she improved by practice in parts of very varying character; her art ripened; her individuality asserted itself; and she acquired authority, the precious quality which adds command to charm.

It was in the 'Taming of the Shrew' that she first asserted this authority with compelling amplitude and assurance. When she rushed on the stage in her wrath, with her flaming gown and her hair flaming above it, she was a superb spectacle of youthful energy, a magnificent animal in a magnificent rage. And it was as Kate the curst that she took London by storm and was rewarded by a fervor of appreciation more exalted than any she had received in New York. Over here we had seen her climbing the ladder, and over there they beheld her at the summit of her artistry. We had the full value of her later mastery shadowed by our recollection of her earlier novitiate. The British might be less than half-hearted in its liking for Daly's idiosyncratic rearrangement of Shakspere's text, but it was whole-hearted in its acknowledgment of Ada Rehan's genius—a large word which I prefer to use with caution but which the enthusiastic Henley applied to Ada Rehan without hesitation. The British were captivated both by her personality and by her power of impersonating.

I do not mean to suggest that Katherine was the best of her Shaksperian performances, but it was the first in which she triumphed. Her Rosalind was delightful in its playfulness and its tenderness; it was blithe and buoyant and above all womanly; it was without taint of self-consciousness and with unfailing enjoyment of the situation. Her Rosalind was fitly companioned by John Drew's Orlando, which was one of the most satisfactory it has ever been my privilege to admire. Indeed, the full effect of Ada Rehan's Rosalind was due in a measure to the fact that John Drew's Orlando accepted Ganymede as a lad and never allowed us to suppose that he suspected all the time that this lad was his very Rosalind. I have elsewhere recorded that Ada Rehan's Portia gave us a new and truer and more effective rendering of the "Quality of Mercy" speech than we had ever had before; she did not make it an elocutionary stunt, as is the wont of most actresses; she spoke it as a direct appeal to Shylock, pausing between sentences in the vain hope that her words might soften his hard heart. And I may add now that her voice was vibrant and melodious; and that she had mastered the difficulties of blank verse, never chopping it into halting prose and never weakly falling into singsong.

In the fall of 1887 Daly asked me to aid him in editing 'A Portfolio of Players,' a privately printed volume containing a score of photogravure portraits of the leading members of his company, with brief commentaries by H. C. Bunner, E. A. Dithmar, Laurence Hutton, William Winter and myself. My own tribute to the irrepressible and irresistible fun of Miss Rehan in her repetition of an empty song called 'Miss Jenny O'Jones' was a little too brief to fill out the space allotted to it; and when Daly wrote asking me to lengthen it a little, he called my attention to "the marvelous versatility and range of Miss Rehan—a range not reached by any living actress"; and he pointed out also "her womanliness in all." And this was before she had revealed the deeper and broader gifts in impersonations of Rosalind and Viola, Portia and Lady Teazle. She grew in stature with the years and she ripened as the seasons rolled around, until at the end there was no rival who had essayed so many and so diverse parts and who had done them all so well.

Charles Lamb thought it a consolation for growing old that he had seen the 'School for Scandal' in all the glory of its original cast; and we who were witnesses of the splendid days of Daly's Theater have a similar solace. To 'A Portfolio of Players' Daumer contributed an epilog addressed 'To a Reader of the Twenty-first Century.'

> "'A Daly private print'"—a chaste
> Example of our fathers' taste.
> They made books *then*—who can, in our
> Degenerate days of—magnet—power?

194

See—Ada Rehan, Fisher, Drew,
Dame Gilbert, Lewis—through and through
The sharp-cut plates are clear as new.
Then comes the old, the tardy praise—
"Those were the drama's palmy days."

But We?—You'll see the shadow—now
To us these living creatures bow,
For us they smile—for us they feign
Or love or hatred, scorn or pain;
For us this white breast heaves—this voice
Makes hearts too young too much rejoice;
For us those splendid eyes are lit;
For us awakes embodied wit;
For us the music and the light—
The listening faces, flushed and bright,
The glow, the passion and the dream—
To you—how far it all must seem!

V

THE company which Daly managed in each
of his theaters was a stock company remaining
substantially the same year after year. It stood
ready to play comedy or tragedy, melodrama or
farce, social drama or comic opera. Sometimes
it lent its support to stars, Mrs. Scott-Siddons,
Charles J. Mathews, Edwin Booth; but for the
most part it was able to do without these expensive interlopers. It was so numerous in its
early seasons that it could give the 'School for
Scandal' in New York while its unemployed

members went to Newark to present 'London Assurance.' This was sheer extravagance, as Daly found to his cost; and when he opened Daly's Theater at Broadway and 30th Street, he was more cautious, and he relied mainly on the famous "Daly quartet"—Ada Rehan and John Drew, Mrs. G. H. Gilbert and James Lewis—who played into each other's hands with unfailing loyalty and who profited by Daly's extraordinary skill in stage-management.

He loved the theater; he lived in it; he was never so happy as when he was directing a rehearsal; he was intensely interested in his work and untiring in his devotion to it. He delighted in his control of what was really a training-school for actors; and he was a strict disciplinarian, exacting complete compliance with his will. He had a marvelous understanding of the stage; and he knew how to perceive the special gifts of his actors and how to develop these gifts. It is noteworthy that those who submitted to his guidance improved while they were subject to his control and that they ceased to advance in their art when they left him. Of course, his judgment was sometimes at fault and his taste was not always impeccable. But he abides as one of the significant figures in the history of the American theater.

No member of his company had been with

him longer than Mrs. G. H. Gilbert, who had appeared in the opening performance of Daly's first season in 1869 and who remained with him till his death in 1899. She was ready to play any kind of part in any kind of play, from Mrs. Candour in the 'School for Scandal' to the Infant Phenomenon in a little sketch taken from an episode in 'Nicholas Nickleby.' She did not like to be out of the bill; and therefore she was willing to accept the most insignificant parts; for example, Curtis, one of the servants in the 'Taming of the Shrew,' a character which appears only in one scene and which has little to do in that solitary appearance. She knew that Daly was always doing his best for her; and he knew that she would always do her best for him.

Altho she was most favorably known by her impersonation of comic characters, she had a dramatic power unknown to those who saw her only in her later years. It is more than half-a-century now since the first night of 'Man and Wife,' and yet I can visualize again the thrill which ran through me when I beheld the sinister figure of Hester Dethridge silently gliding down the stage for some evil purpose that I can no longer remember. I recall that in 'Froufrou' only a few months earlier she had been miscast as a woman of the world; but altho this

197

character was out of her line, she was at least adequate.

I have mentioned her Mrs. Candour and I regret to have to say that it was not one of her most satisfactory efforts; it was a little too dry, perhaps even a little too intellectual; it lacked the unction and the broad humor which ought to characterize the gossip-monger and mischief-maker of Sheridan's comedy. Yet she looked the part to perfection; and she danced in the minuet with the perfect grace which was always hers. She had been a professional dancer in her youth; and this early experience stood her in good stead when she appeared as Mme. Pier-rot in that ever-delightful pantomime the 'Enfant Prodigue.' Thanks to her youthful training in the ballet, pantomime was an art of which she was a past mistress. Here she had the advantage over Ada Rehan, who played Pierrot, and who always seemed to be wanting to talk and who employed gesture only because she could not speak, whereas Mrs. Gilbert used gesture as speech.

Mrs. Gilbert was held in affectionate regard by all the members of the Daly company. She was always gracious and encouraging to the newcomers. From her varied experience she was able to be helpful to the young folks who were trying their wings; and she often guarded them from the pitfalls into which they might tumble from ignorance of the traditions. She was as cheerful as she was helpful. She appeared to best advantage when she was playing over against James Lewis, whose humor was akin to hers, dry, restrained and clear-cut. She survived this partner of her toils as she survived Daly. Thereafter her occupation was gone; and altho Clyde Fitch adapted 'Grandma' specially for her and not unsuccessfully, she did not linger long on the stage. As I "squeeze the sponge of the memory" (to borrow a phrase from Henry James) and as I try to call the list of the countless parts in which she appeared, I am inclined to the opinion that she was the most varied and the most accomplished impersonator of old women that it has been my good fortune to observe. She had her limitations, no doubt; but in her own field she was unexcelled.

VI

It has always been a puzzle to me that there are so few notable performers of "old women." I can name half-a-dozen brilliant actresses as Lady Teazle, while I should be hard put to it to cite more than one or two fairly satisfactory renditions of Mrs. Malaprop and Mrs. Candour. Every season there appear young actresses of real promise; and some of these persevere and fulfil expectation; but very few of them, even after the lapse of twoscore years on the stage, are able to confirm their earlier reputation by developing from leading ladies into old women. I suppose that they prefer to retire rather than to play mothers instead of daughters. Mostly they shrink from facing the fact of old age.

It is true that Ellen Terry, once triumphantly acclaimed as Juliet, has since been willing to express the rich and oily humor of Juliet's nurse. More often than not the actress who has continued to appear as the youthful heroine, year after year and even decade after decade, refuses to acknowledge the march of time and insists on believing herself to be as young as she feels.

It is Legouvé—at least, I think it was in the pages of this charming chronicler of the French stage in the middle of the nineteenth century that I found the story—it is to Legouvé that I owe a characteristic tale of Mlle. Mars, whose advancing years did not prevent her from conveying the impression of youth by sheer force of art, far more convincingly than could be done by actresses thirty years younger than she. After she was fifty she refused to relinquish the girls of twenty to the girls who were twenty. She was held in such high esteem by her comrades of the Comédie-Française that no one of them was willing to hint to her that she ought thereafter to content herself with more mature characters. When that most ingenious of playwrights, Eugène Scribe, was appealed to, he volunteered to help them out. He wrote a little piece about a young grandmother who was so charming that she was the successful rival of her own granddaughter. But when he read the comedy to Mlle. Mars, she said that she would be delighted to act in it—"but who is there to play the grandmother?"

Forty years ago and more there were two actresses, one in Great Britain and the other in the United States, who brought to the performance of old women the mastery of effect which they had acquired in the impersonation of leading ladies. Mrs. Sterling had been the original Peg Woffington in 'Masks and Faces'; and Mrs. John Drew had been accepted as one of the best of Lady Teazles. At almost the same time they appeared one in London and one in New York as Mrs. Malaprop. Both of them won the plaudits of the public, but by totally different methods. Both had had authority; both were popular favorites, assured of a welcome in whatever they undertook; both knew all the traditions of Old Comedy; and there the resemblance ended.

Mrs. Sterling was a mistress of all the bolder

devices for arousing laughter; she sought broad effects; she splashed on her color with an unsparing hand as tho she could not trust the intelligence of the spectators. I do not dare to be rude enough to hint that she clowned the part; yet I cannot find any other term fit to describe her method. In her hands Mrs. Malaprop was not a lady and not a finely drawn character; rather was she a caricature, intensely self-conscious of her verbal blunders. As the time came for one of them to be delivered, she visibly braced herself for effort, as tho saying to the audience, "I'm Mrs. Malaprop and here is another malapropism. It's a good one, I assure you. You really can't help laughing at it. Are you ready for it?" Then she hurled it at the spectators, waiting for the outburst of laughter, and smiling in comic complicity with them, as if assuring them that it was a good one, wasn't it?

When Mrs. Drew played Mrs. Malaprop she lifted the part from low comedy to high comedy. Sheridan's figure of fun ceased to be a caricature and became a deftly etched character, more human and more humorous. Mrs. Drew's Mrs. Malaprop was a woman educated beyond her intelligence and puffed with pride in her little learning. She was serenely unconscious that there was any such things as malapropisms, and she delivered each of them with evident delight in her "nice derangement of epitaphs," letting us share in her joy that she had hit upon exactly the right word, the only word, the word that she alone could provide. Every malapropism was a fresh invention of hers; she made us feel that it had just occurred to her; and thus she produced the illusion of spontaneity. She exhibited the perfected art which seemed like nature, because it was able to conceal its processes. As a result of this subtler reading of the lines and of this more accurate conception of the part, Mrs. Drew's Mrs. Malaprop was really more effective than Mrs. Sterling's. If I may trust my memory after more than two-score years, the laughter it evoked was both heartier and more abundant.

In his 'Autobiography,' worthy to stand by the side of Colley Cibber's incomparable 'Apology,' Joseph Jefferson makes us share the pleasure he had in acting with Mrs. Drew in the 'Rivals,' and he records that she was the inventor of a novel piece of business. Mrs. Malaprop is deeply disgusted with the persistence of her niece, Lydia Languish, in loving "Ensign Beverley." She says, "Oh, it gives me the hydrostatics to such a degree! I thought she had persisted from corresponding with him; but, behold, this very day, I have interceded another letter from the fellow; I believe I have it in my pocket." Then Mrs. Drew used to search in her voluminous pocket for the missive and by mistake to take out the letter of Sir Lucius O'Trigger. Then discovering her error and in great confusion she pulled forth the epistle which Captain Absolute recognizes to his immediate embarrassment. The ingenuity of this is as evident as its propriety is indisputable. It is a happy suggestion which Sheridan, we may be sure, would have adopted with a gratitude equal to that of the younger Dumas when he accepted a similar improvement due to Eleanora Duse's fine dramatic instinct.

"Those were the drama's palmy days"; and no doubt our grandchildren will say the same of ours.

(1923)

XI

THE ART OF ACTING

XI

THE ART OF ACTING

I

WHEN George Henry Lewes collected into an invaluable little volume his scattered essays 'On Actors and the Art of Acting' he prefixt a prefatory letter to Anthony Trollope, wherein he dwelt on the ignorance of the fundamental basis of the actor's art wide-spread even among men of culture, who would have held it disgraceful to be as ill-informed about the principles of any of the kindred arts. "I have heard those," he wrote, "for whose opinions in other directions my respect is great, utter judgments on this subject which proved that they had not even a suspicion of what the art of acting really is. Whether they blamed or praised, the grounds which they advanced for praise or blame were often questionable."

In the twoscore years since Lewes made this sweeping assertion the actor has attracted more and more attention; the theater has again established its importance both in Great Britain and the United States; and the drama has shown many signs that it is likely to recover its lost ground among the peoples that speak English. And yet the general ignorance in regard to the art of acting is scarcely less than it was when Lewes was comparing Edmund Kean with Rachel and recording his first impressions of Salvini. A knowledge of the principles of the art is no more widely diffused now than it was when the staple play of the English stage was a mangled and misleading adaptation from the French.

Unthinking spectators will always fail to give a thought to the unseen dramatist, and they will always confuse the actor with the character he is personating. They will applaud the lovely heroine, because they sympathize with her sufferings or her sentiments, wholly regardless of the artistic accomplishment of the actress who impersonates her; and they will hiss the unsightly villain, whom they detest for his evil intent, even tho the actor taking the part may be the most skilful of the performers. They would discover nothing absurd in the remark of a certain drummer, once made to a distinguished comedian: "Mr. Drew, I don't see how you manage to think of so many clever things to say on the stage. I wish I could learn to do that. It would be mighty useful to me in my business."

And not only unthinking spectators are capable of absurdities of this sort, for a similar ignorance is sometimes revealed even by those who are permitted to write theatrical notices in the newspapers. Whoever has occasion to read many of these reports must have seen more than one passage in which the reviewer credited the actor with the ingenuity which the playwright had bestowed on the character. For example, the account of the first performance of a British farce which appeared in one of the New York papers a few years ago stated that "Miss Blank was excellent; in fact, she did quite the cleverest thing in the play when she was quick-witted enough to arrange the furniture so as to deceive the officers of the law." Blunders as flagrant as this are not common, of course; but that they occur at all is evidence of a disheartening misunderstanding of the art of the stage.

That gross misconceptions of this sort should actually get into print is evidence also of a general belief that dramatic reviewing is easy, and that anybody may be trusted to write a theatrical notice, however little he knows about the theater. It may be admitted possibly that a descriptive paragraph or two can be considered quite sufficient for the most of the entertainments offered in our playhouses,—entertainments often satisfactory, each in its own fashion, and yet not demanding serious consideration. But circumstances change when an important new play is produced. Then the task of the dramatic reviewer may be both difficult and delicate, since he has to form an opinion as to the merits of the play itself, which he can know only through this single performance, and at the same time to judge the actors also as they appear in this half-known piece. In other words, he can see the play only through the players, as he can see the performers only through the piece; and either medium may refract so that he shall get a false image.

Sometimes a play of less than average merit may be saved by superior acting, or even by the surpassing personal appeal of the chief actor or actress. The special vocabulary of the theater recognizes this; and it describes certain characters as "parts that play themselves," and certain plays as "actor-proof," meaning thereby that these parts and these plays are likely to please the public even if they are inadequately performed. The stage-folk also know certain characters as "ungrateful parts," recognizing that even the best acting cannot make them satisfactory to the performer or to the spectator. And the French go further: they speak of a "false good part," meaning thereby a part which appears to be prominent and important but which is not as rich as it seems, altho its real poverty is often not revealed even to the actor himself until the actual performance. These are subtleties of the histrionic art which are never suspected by the ordinary playgoer, who comes to the theater in search of unthinking recreation. But they need to be mastered by every critic of the acted drama.

II

PROBABLY the ordinary playgoer would be swift to accept the first of two definitions once proposed by Bronson Howard: "The art of acting is the art of moving, speaking, and appearing on the stage as the character assumed would move, speak, and appear in real life, under the circumstances indicated in the play." As he suggested, this appears to be a reasonable definition; but, as he went on to explain, it is "absolutely and radically false," because it leaves out the one essential word. It ought to read: "The art of acting is the art of *seeming* to move, speak, and appear on the stage as the character assumed moves, speaks, and appears in real life, under the circumstances indicated in the play." And the experienced dramatist commented on this second definition and explained that "the actor's art is to make the people in an audience, some of them a hundred feet or more away, *think* that he is moving, speaking, and appearing like the character assumed; and, in nine cases out of ten, the only way to make them think so is *not* to be doing it; to be doing something else."

And in his helpful discussion of his own calling, 'Art and the Actor,' Coquelin insisted on the same point. You may do what you please in your effort to attain the utmost or realism in scenery and in furniture, the stage will ever remain the stage, and it cannot be the real thing. "You are in the theater," the great French actor declared, "and not in the street or at home. If you put on the stage the action of the street or the home, there will result very much what would happen if you were to put a life-sized statue on top of a column: it would no longer seem to be life-sized."

When the sculptor is modeling a statue for the top of a column or for the pediment of a monumental edifice, to be seen only from below, he proportions it to this lofty height, very differently from the way in which he would deal with the same figure if it had to stand by itself on a low pedestal in an open square. So the actor has to adjust his representation of reality to the large theater, so much larger than the room in which the character is supposed to stand. He has to change his scale, to translate the actual reality into the semblance of reality. He can seem real only by not sticking absolutely to the facts. Lewes quoted from the diary of the French comedian Molé a note to the effect that this actor, one evening, was not satisfied with his work, since he had let himself go and had been "too much the character itself" and no longer the actor playing it: "I was real as I would have been at home; I ought to have been real in another way, in accord with the perspective of the theater." This suggests an explanation of the fact that a lady who has stept from society to the stage may appear almost unladylike as an actress, altho in her own home she might be an accomplished woman of the world. She cannot *seem* what she really *is* because she does not understand the perspective of the theater.

III

To get a firm grasp of the principles of the art of acting is at least as difficult as it is to seize those of the art of painting, and the inquirer can find most profit in conference with the actual practitioners of the art. Much of the chatter about painters and painting is futile and foolish; and so is most of the chatter about actors and acting. But we can listen with as much pleasure as profit when the artists themselves are willing to talk about their art, to discuss their own way of working, and to reveal the secrets of the craft. As John La Farge once declared, what the artist "has to say about himself and his art is of the utmost use, and, in fact, is the only authority. All people interested, that is to say, all real students, . . . must make the effort to learn in any direction, whatever it may be,—through the wording of the teachers,"—who are also practitioners of the art.

So we learn best about painting from La Farge himself, and from Fromentin, and from a few other painters who happen also to have the critical faculty and the gift of exposition. And in like manner we can find our profit in what the actors have to say about their own art,—not in formal disquisition, but in suggestive discussion of their fellow craftsmen. It is true that one actor,—Samson,—who was Rachel's trainer, a most finished comedian, prepared a set treatise on the histrionic art; but his didactic poem, on the model of Horace's 'Art of Poetry,' has never been rendered into English. But we have the incomparable 'Apology for the Life of Colley Cibber,' and the illuminating 'Autobiography' of Joseph Jefferson, and the stimulating lecture on the art of the actor by Coquelin, the most accomplished of comedians in the final years of the nineteenth century. And then there is the little collection of essays by George Henry Lewes, an actor himself, a playwright also, and the son of an actor, with an inherited insight into the practice of the profession.

These are more useful than the works of the professed critics of the theater, altho there is much to be gleaned here and there in the writings of Lamb and Hazlitt, in the two solid tomes devoted to the chief figures of the contemporary French stage by the late Francisque Sarcey, and in the ingenious inquiry of Mr. William Archer, which he called 'Masks or Faces,' and in which he collected the evidence for and against Diderot's 'Paradox'—that the actor must not feel too acutely the emotion he is depicting. Not to be overlooked are the pregnant words of the playwrights also: Shakspere's advice to the Players in 'Hamlet,' Molière's counsel to his own comrades in the 'Impromptu of Versailles,' and Legouvé's excellent papers on Rachel and Ristori. The relation of the dramaturgic art to the histrionic must ever be very close; and the dramatist has perforce to acquire a certain knowledge of the actors' technic, or else he will not be able properly to prepare what he is devising for their use.

IV

THE dramatic poet always intends his works for the stage itself; he plans them to be performed before an audience, in a theater, and by actors. Therefore he is ever taking account of the spectators, and of their prejudices and of their predilections; he is always careful to adjust his work to the actual conditions of the theater of his own time; and he utilizes to the utmost the special qualifications of the actors who are to take part in the performance. A great poet cannot write a play without considering the actor's art, any more than he can write a lyric to be set to music without considering the vocalist's art. Shelley is a far finer lyrist than Moore, but the Irish bard sang his songs into being, and their open vowels are ever a delight to the singer; whereas the English poet, giving little thought to the musician, filled his lyrics with consonants which close the mouth. "The stage is to the prose-drama," so Henry James once remarked, "what the time is to the song, or the concrete case to the general law."

It is at his peril that the playwright does not take the player into account. No one of the great dramatists, it is well to remember, has ever failed to maintain cordial relations with

216

the several performers of his plays. Better than any one else, the great dramatist knew how much he might be indebted to the actors, to their skill, to their sympathy, and to their loyalty. Sometimes, it is true, we find an author who has sought success on the stage without attaining the aim of his ambition, allowing himself to express an unfavorable opinion of actors as a class. Daudet, for one, was sharp in his detection and delineation of their defects. But the real playwrights are glad ever to show their hearty appreciation of the coöperation they have received from the actor who helped to reveal the vitality of their works. Some of them are willing to go as far as Voltaire went after Mlle. Clairon had impersonated his 'Electra,' when he declared, "It is not I who did that;—she did it! She has really *created* the character!"

Nor is this an exaggeration, a mere empty compliment. That playwright is without wide experience who has not had the unexpected pleasure of beholding one of his characters transformed by an actor, who charged it with a meaning and a purpose, a variety and a veracity, that the author himself did not suspect and that he had not consciously intended. This transformation may have been caused by the artistic insight of the performer, or it may have been due simply to his personality. Sometimes a part is thus transfigured merely by the physical fitness of the actor for the character. For it is not only the personality of the actor which affects his art: it is also his actual person. The tools of his trade are the members of his own body. His hands and his arms, his walk and his gesture, the glance of his eye and the tones of his voice,—these are the implements of his art, these are his chisel and his marble, his brushes, his palette, and his canvas.

V

HE acts with his own person, and that must ever be the material of his art. He is fortunate, indeed, if he happens to be young and handsome, strong of limb and manly in bearing, with expressive eyes and a moving voice. These natural gifts will carry him along, if only he can acquire even a slight acquaintance with the elements of his art. Many a pretty woman has gone on the stage and won immediate popularity by her personal charm alone, by the compelling power of her youth, her grace, and her beauty. This is what Fanny Kemble did; and yet she admitted at once the justice of Macready's assertion that she did not know the rudiments of her profession. Descended from a race of artists, the daughter of Charles Kemble recognized that she herself was only an amateur. Another lady who had met with a similar success for similar reasons, but who married and gave up the theater after two or three years of acting, once confessed to me, later in life, that it was only toward the end of her brief career on the stage that she had begun to find out how she made her effects, learning doubtfully how to control them and how to repeat them night after night. That is to say, the actress was just learning the rudiments of her profession, altho the woman had long won by her personal attraction a prosperous popularity in the theater.

This it is that chiefly distinguishes the actors from all other artists,—that they must do their work with their own persons and in public. The poet may retire to an ivory tower far away, and the painter may prefer a remote solitude; they separate what they do from themselves, and they send this away. They are not present when we read the poem or see the picture. They do not come into direct contact with us, and they may ignore us, if they see fit. But the actor must work in the presence of the public, and the material of his art is himself. And this again accounts for the acuter sensitiveness of the actor to criticism. It is easy enough to discuss what the poet has done, or the painter, without personal comment. But how is it possible to separate the art of the actor from his personality? How can the artist and the man be disentangled? How may an adverse criticism on the performance of a part avoid the appearance of an adverse criticism on the personal characteristics of the human being who has put himself inside the character? Perhaps it might be achieved by a critic of extraordinary skill and delicacy; but it is too much to expect from the average theatrical reviewer.

It was a wise appreciation of this fact which led Edwin Booth to recommend the permanent debarring of the professed theatrical reviewer from membership in The Players, the club which he founded for his own profession and for the practitioners of the allied arts of literature, painting, sculpture, architecture, and music. Even the journalist, as such, is not excluded, so long as he will refrain from the discussion of contemporary actors. The literary critic is admitted, since any author must be strangely thin-skinned who cannot sit at meat with the writer of an adverse review; and the critic of painting is made welcome, since the painter and his work are easily separable. But the histrionic critic must remain outside the doors of The Players since he cannot, whatever his good-will, deal with the actor without lapsing into personal comment on the man. This rule of The

Players is an unwritten law only, but it is always
obeyed; and more than one member attracted
to theatrical reviewing has had reluctantly to
renounce the privilege of being a Player. This
wise rule has only one disadvantage: by keep-
ing the actor and the critic apart it lessens the
opportunity of the latter to learn more about
the art of the former.

VI

To win a fair proportion of popular approval
an actor needs only an attractive personality
and also a modicum of the mimetic faculty,—
of the special aptitude for the stage, which is
as distinct a gift as the aptitude for story-telling,
or for making verses, or for acquiring money.
The successful actor may happen also to be a
man of wide intelligence, as Garrick was, and
Coquelin also; but he is no more likely to have
an acute intellect than is a successful novelist
or a successful business man. The men who
make money and the men who write popular
novels may or may not be possessed of remarkable mental ability; they have succeeded rather
by virtue of their special aptitude for story-
telling or for money-making. The special aptitude of the actor may be accompanied by ability
in other directions; but the possession of the

221

special aptitude is not evidence that he has also the wider intelligence.

Just as Paul Morphy was the foremost of chess-players, but in other respects only a man of ordinary capacity, so an actor of high rank may be no more brilliant than the average man. Mrs. Siddons was the greatest of Lady Macbeths, with an incomparable skill in sounding the unseen depths of that tragic figure; but the essay she wrote on the subject is almost valueless. Salvini was the greatest of Othellos, with a lofty largeness of imaginative interpretation; but his critical papers on the part do not display any special insight. Mrs. Siddons and Salvini were dowered with the special aptitude of acting, and they cultivated this gift loyally and diligently; but outside of their acting they were only ordinary mortals.

Probably this is what Lewes had in mind when he asserted that "people generally overrate a fine actor's genius, and underrate his trained skill. They are apt to credit him with a power of intellectual conception and poetic creation to which he has really a very slight claim, and fail to recognize all the difficulties which his artistic training has enabled him to master." What the actor needs, if he is to rise high in his calling, is not general intelligence but the special intelligence of his own art, the intuitive understanding of its possibilities and of its limitations, the clear insight into its principles and the power swiftly to apply them. That he should always be conscious of the full effect of what he does, that he should always know just why he does it,—this is not at all necessary, for often the best work of the artist is instinctive. He does what he does because that is indeed the only way for him to do it. There is no need that he should be conscious of his processes, or that he should be able to trace the steps that led him to the satisfactory result. Poe is not a greater poet because he has analyzed the succession of motives which had led him to the composition of the 'Raven.'

Like all other artists, the actor is greatest in his achievement when he has builded better than he knew. His native aptitude and his artistic training enable him to produce an impression which often seems to be the result of pure intellectual power. Planché has an anecdote in point: The day after the first performance of a play of his in which a certain comedian had given an intelligent and impressive performance of a leading character, this actor applied to the author for the loan of the manuscript, explaining that he had been absent when the play had been read to the company and he did not really "know what it was all about."

And yet, his innate gift and his skill in his own profession had permitted him to profit by the hints of the stage-manager at rehearsal, and so to deliver the words of his part as to suggest a keen intellectual appreciation of the action, even if he did not "know what it was all about." He had not had wit enough to find out the story of the play before he acted in it; and yet when he acted it he seemed to display ample intelligence.

VII

In one of M. Jean Richepin's stories of stage-life there is a veracious portrait of a broken-down actor so enamored of his art that he must ever be teaching it, wherefore he has gathered about him a group of ambitious urchins whom he instructs in acting and to whom he imparts the principles of the craft. He has the actor's frequent contempt for the mere author of the play, and he impresses on his young pupils that they are always to go behind the words of their parts to the emotions evoked by the situation itself, since it is the duty of the actor to express these emotions richly and completely, no matter how poorly and meagerly the author may have voiced them. Even if the words happen to be inadequate or halting, the actor must take care to convey the sentiment fully to the audience.

And then, to emphasize the unimportance of the mere word, the old instructor picked out a common phrase—indeed, one of the vulgarest of all —and bade his little pupils repeat that single phrase with the feeling proper to each of a series of situations,—making love to a lady, defying a rival, blessing a child, and saying farewell to a dying mother. He made them employ always this same vulgar phrase, surcharging it with the full emotion belonging to each of these several actions.

Altho there is more than a hint of caricature in M. Richepin's sketch, the method of his old comedian is praiseworthy; it is by such emotional gymnastic as this that the performer acquires flexibility. The actor needs to have under control not only his gestures and his tones, but all other means of simulating sensibility; and these should be ready for use at all times, wholly independent of the words of the text. He must be able so to breathe "Mesopotamia" that it shall seem to be a blessed word, indeed. The Italian tragedian Ernesto Rossi used to assert that "a great actor is independent of the poet, because the supreme essence of feeling does not reside in prose or in verse, but in the accent with which it is delivered."

This is not a specimen of professional vainglory, altho it may have that appearance. It is only the overstatement of a fact. Rossi himself

used to adduce as evidence in its behalf a little
story. He was having supper one evening at
Padua with half-a-dozen fellow actors, and they
fell into discussion of their own art and of its
possibilities. One of them picked up the bill of
fare and declared his intention of reading this
barren list so pathetically as to bring tears to
their eyes. The other actors refused to believe
that this was possible; they were not credulous
spectators; they were hardened to every trick
of the trade; and they smiled at his proposal.
The first words he read simply, rising soon to a
large dignity of utterance that veiled the com-
monplace syllables. Then his rich, full voice
began to tremble as if with fear, and to quiver
at length as tho the soul of the speaker was
pierced with poignant agony. Despite the re-
pugnant words, which ceased to be perceived
clearly, the sweeping emotions with which his
tones were charged proved to be irresistibly
contagious; and long before he had read to the
end of the bill of fare, his comrades found themselves looking at each other with tears rolling
down their cheeks.

VIII

THE French author of the pleasant book
about the contemporary Italian stage from which

this little story has been borrowed failed to record the name of the actor who was the hero of
Rossi's anecdote, and who, very likely, was not
a performer of high rank. Even if he had at
his command the perfect control of a beautiful
voice, he may have been devoid of other necessary implements of his art. Above all, he may
have lacked that "intelligence of his profession"
which alone would enable him to employ these
implements to best advantage. The mere possession of all the tools of his trade does not of
itself make the craftsman. The means of expression, however ample and however varied,
are useless unless there is something to express,
—and something which it is worth while to express.

Many an actor strong in execution is weak
in conception. He does not know what it is
best for him to do, tho he knows how to do it
when this is shown to him. He needs guidance
and he cannot steer himself, altho he is certain
to make a swift trip if only his course is directed
by a wiser head. Here is the duty and the opportunity of the dramatist himself, or of the
producer of the play, who need not be much
of an actor, but who must know how the play
ought to be acted in every part, and who can
suggest to the several performers the various
effects they are to accomplish. It may sound

227

like a paradox to assert that the author of a play, who often cannot act at all, can yet teach the actors who are his masters in this art; but this is exactly what he may have to do. Sardou told us that he schooled Anaïs Fargueil in many of the effects he had studied in Ristori's acting.

Sometimes, it is true, the playwright may be also an accomplished actor, and the result of this combination is generally very advantageous. A play of Mr. Gillette's or of the late James A. Herne's, in which the author himself acted, appeared always to be performed by comedians of unusual intelligence. Sometimes the manager of the theater, or the stage-manager who brings out plays, has this power of suggesting and controlling and guiding. Sometimes even performers of the highest distinction have been indebted to a teacher who lighted the path that else they would have trodden in darkness. This dependence of the performer on the trainer has been excellently seized by Thackeray in 'Pendennis,' wherein we are shown how Little Bowes the fiddler had taught the lovely Miss Fotheringay,—how he was the organist and how she was the instrument whose music has been evoked by him, hidden and unsuspected.

Finer actresses by far than the adored Miss Fotheringay have owed much to a trainer in the background. Even the great Mrs. Siddons

228

was indebted for many of her effects to the inventive brain of her brother, John Philip Kemble. The great Rachel, again, was the pupil of Samson, a little comic actor, who yet was able to teach her how to attain to the loftiest heights of tragedy. She used to say that she was "lame on one side" until Samson had shown her what to do with a part. Legouvé has recorded how she turned to Samson during one of the rehearsals of 'Adrienne Lecouvreur' and, in the presence of her assembled comrades, expressed her gratitude to him, who had shown her how to get the best out of herself.

Every one at all familiar with the inner history of the stage in Great Britain and the United States during the last quarter of the nineteenth century is aware that two of the actresses who held a foremost position in the theater of both countries were immensely indebted to the constant counsel of two of their professional associates. They had each of them, not exactly a Little Bowes in the background, but a Samson, who guided them and who trained them to get the utmost out of their histrionic gift. To the unthinking spectators in the theaters of London and New York the performances of these charming actresses appeared to be singularly spontaneous and freely individual. Yet this free spontaneity was the result of their being able to take a hint, to assimilate the suggestion they received, and to profit by it, each in her own fashion and in accord with her own temperament. Each of them was an emotional instrument, played on by a far keener artistic intelligence than her own.

IX

WHEN the keen artistic intelligence and the rich emotional instrument happen to be in the possession of the same person, then the world is likely to have another great actor. The intelligence alone will not suffice, or else Shakspere would have been the foremost actor of his day, and not Burbage. The emotion alone will not do it, unless it can express itself adequately by voice and look and gesture,—"the actor's symbols," as Lewes calls them, through which he makes intelligible the emotions of the character he is personating. "No amount of sensibility will avail unless it can express itself adequately by these symbols. It is not enough for an actor to *feel*: he must *represent*. He must express his feelings in symbols universally intelligible and affecting."

If we may rely on the testimony of Lewes himself, actors as prominent as Macready and Charles Kean, men of intelligence and of character both of them, did not really attain to the highest altitudes of their art, because of their defective control of these symbols, the result of purely physical disadvantages. As we study the long annals of the theater, striving to ascertain what player most certainly combined in himself all the attributes of a truly great actor, we are likely to be led to the conclusion that no one has a better claim to the supreme chieftainship of the histrionic art than David Garrick, equally powerful in comedy and in tragedy, and as warmly welcomed in France as he was highly esteemed in England:

As an actor, confessed without rival to shine:
As a wit, if not first, in the very first line.

In our own day we have been fortunate in the privilege of studying two of the masters of the stage,—Jefferson and Coquelin,—probably as accomplished and as richly endowed as any of their predecessors in the theater, gifted by nature and trained by art. Having something within them to express, and possessing perfect command of the symbols of expression, they had also, each of them, wide cultivation, unusual intelligence, and delightful individuality.

X

DAVID GARRICK may have been the greatest
actor the world has ever seen; but what is he
to-day but a faint memory—a name in the bio-
graphical dictionaries, and little more? Joseph
Jefferson was the most delightful comedian of
the English-speaking stage at the end of the
nineteenth century; but his fame will fade like
Garrick's, and in a score of years he also will
be but a name, and no longer an alert personality sharp in the recollection of all living playgoers. This swift removal to the limbo of the
vanished is the fate of all actors, however popular in their own day, and however indisputable
their manifold gifts.

And this fate the actor shares with all performers,—orators, vocalists, and instrumental-
ists. It is a fate from which the practitioners of
the other arts are preserved by the fact that
their works may live after them, whereas the
performers can leave nothing behind them but
the splendid recollection that may linger in the
memories of those who beheld the performance.
Goldsmith was the friend of Garrick; and there
are thousands to-day who have enjoyed the
quaint simplicity of the 'Vicar of Wakefield,'
and to whom therefore Goldsmith is something
more than a mere name. Macready was the

friend of Bulwer-Lytton, who wrote for him the 'Lady of Lyons' and 'Richelieu'; but the actor left the stage more than half-a-century ago and has been forgotten by the playgoers, who long continued to attend the countless performances of the two plays Macready had originally produced.

The actors are moved often to repeat the pathetic query of Rip when he returned from his sleep of twenty years, "Are we, then, so soon forgot?" And Jefferson himself answered the question in the affirmative. He told Mr. Francis Wilson that Betterton and Garrick, Kean and Mrs. Siddons, "mark milestones in the dramatic pathway, for they lived at a time when literary men wrote sympathetically of the stage, and so their memories are kept alive." He thought that Edwin Booth might be more than a tradition solely because he had founded a club— The Players—whereby his fame would be kept green. When Mr. Wilson then asked him about himself, the shrewd comedian explained that his own 'Autobiography' might serve to rescue him from total oblivion. And he summed up the case and dismissed it finally with the assertion that "the painter, the sculptor, the author, all live in their works after death,—but there is nothing so useless as a dead actor! Acting is a tradition. Actors must have their reward now, in the applause of the public,—or never.

If their names live, it must be because of some extraneous circumstance."

Other distinguished actors have phrased the same thought even more forcibly. Delaunay, for a third of a century the ideal young lover in all the masterpieces of dramatic literature performed at the Théâtre Français, used to liken the actor to the painter in Hoffmann's weird tale, who sat before a blank canvas with an empty brush and yet gave all the touches needed for a true picture. And Lawrence Barrett was fond of repeating an anecdote of Michelangelo. To please some exacting patron or to gratify a whim of his own, the great artist, so it is said, once carved a statue of snow. This may have been the final expression of his plastic genius; but it endured only until the sun shone again. Then it melted swiftly into a shapeless lump, and soon it was gone forever, leaving no record of its powerful beauty. "And this is what the actor does every night," so Barrett was wont to comment; "he is forever carving a statue of snow."

XI

So strong is the instinctive human desire for immortality, so abiding is the wish of man to transmit to those who may come after some testimony of himself, that these regretful utterances of the actors are very natural, indeed. But is their case really as hard as they think it? Has the actor no compensation for the transitoriness of his fame?

And when we seek an honest answer to these questions, we can find one without difficulty. Indeed, we can find two,—one of them obvious enough, and the other perhaps not so evident, but not less suggestive.

The first answer is contained in Jefferson's assertion that "actors must have their reward now, in the applause of the public,—or never." And we all know that actors do have their reward,—an ample reward, pressed down and running over. Both in praise and in cash, the actor is better paid than any other artist. In proportion to his accomplishment, he is greatly overpaid, since the nightly salary of a prima donna far overtops the modest fee of the composer of the opera. The possible earnings of celebrated performers are almost fabulous, now that they can make the whole world tributary. It may be that the pecuniary gains of a very popular actor are not actually greater than those of a very popular novelist or of a very popular portrait-painter. But where there are to-day only one or two novelists and portrait-painters who have attained to this summit of prosperity, there are a dozen or a score of actors and of actresses who are reaping the richest of harvests. And even the rank and file of the histrionic profession are better paid than are the average practitioners of the other arts.

The actor, overpaid in actual money so far as his real ability is concerned, is also unduly rewarded with adulation. In the general ignorance about the art of acting, he is often rated far more highly than he deserves. He is greeted with public acclaim; and he can rejoice in the wide reverberations of a notoriety which is the immediate equivalent of fame. He comes almost in personal contact with his admirers, and they are loud in expressing to him the pleasure he has just given them. Far more directly and far more keenly than any poet or any sculptor can the actor breathe up the incense that is offered to him. And if he happen to be a Kemble, he may have the good fortune to listen while a Campbell declares acting to be the supreme art:

> For ill can Poetry express
>   Full many a tone of thought sublime,
> And painting, mute and motionless,
>   Steals but a glance of Time.
> But by the mighty actor brought,
>   Illusion's perfect triumphs come,—
> Verse ceases to be airy thought,
>   And Sculpture to be dumb.

Even if the actor is not a Kemble and does not receive the homage of a Campbell, even if he is but one of the many stars that twinkle in the theatrical firmament, he has a celebrity denied to other artists. He may expect to be recognized as he passes in the street. He may count on the public familiarity with his name, such as no other artist could hope for. Few of those who throng through the portals of a noble building ever give a thought to the architect whose work it is. Few of those who stand in admiration before a stately statue in a public square ever ask the name of the sculptor who wrought it.

Even in the theater itself only a few of those who sit entranced at the performance of a play know or care to know its authorship. Bronson Howard was once asked how many of the audience that filled the theater at the hundredth performance of one of his plays would be aware that he was the author of the piece they were enjoying; and he answered that he doubted if one in ten of the spectators happened to be acquainted with his name. But at least nine in ten of the spectators knew the names of the stars; and when that piece chanced to be performed later by one of the stock companies, it was advertised as "Robson and Crane's great play, the 'Henrietta.'" So it is that the player

is ever overshadowing the playwright, altho the
actor is but the interpreter of what the author
has created. It is the incalculable advantage
of the actor that "he stands in the suffused
light of emotion kindled by the author," so
Lewes declared, adding that the performer de-
livering "the great thoughts of an impassioned
mind is rewarded as the bearer of glad tidings
is rewarded, tho he may have had nothing to
do with the facts which he narrates."

XII

A CERTAIN rough-and-ready justice there is
in most of the affairs of this life; and by this
those who have their brief hour upon the stage
may profit, like the rest of us. The obvious
compensation for the swift forgetting that may
follow the most renowned actor's withdrawal
from active service in the theater is to be found
in the fact that while he was prominent before
the footlights he was probably more or less overpaid either in approbation or in money, and possibly in both. But there is another compensation less obvious, and indeed wholly overlooked
by those who have discussed the subject. Even
Lewes failed to state it, altho he seems to have
been almost in sight of it.

"It is thought a hardship that great actors

in quitting the stage can leave no monument more solid than a name," so Lewes wrote commenting on the retirement of Macready. "The painter leaves behind him pictures to attest his power; the author leaves behind him books; the actor leaves only a tradition. The curtain falls —the artist is annihilated. Succeeding generations may be told of his genius; none can test it." But Lewes did not see the significance of these final words "none can test it." They suggest that in one respect, at least, the actor may be more fortunate than any other artist. His fame in the future depends absolutely on the reputation which he achieved while he was alive and active in his profession. From that pedestal he can never be deposed. On that height he is secure, whatever the changes of critical theory and whatever the vagaries of public opinion. For him the judgment of his contemporaries is final; and posterity has no court of appeal. The election on the face of the returns must stand; and it can never be voided later, since the ballots have been destroyed.

This is a security of tenure possessed by no painter and by no poet, whose works survive to be valued anew by the changing standards of successive generations. Painters exalted in one century as indisputable masters have been cast down in another century and denounced

239

as mere pretenders. Pope was acclaimed in his own day as the greatest of English poets, only to be disdained in a few score years as an adroit versifier, a mere wit, not fairly to be termed a poet at all. From these vicissitudes of criticism the actor is preserved; his fame cannot be impeached. No critic can move for a retrial of Garrick; the witnesses are all dead; the case is closed; the decision stands forever. "Succeeding generations may be told of his genius; none can test it";—and because none can test it, succeeding generations must accept what they have been told. Garrick painted his picture with an empty brush, it is true, and he had to carve his statue in the snow; and therefore neither the picture nor the statue can ever be seen again by unfriendly eyes. The skill of the artist cannot be proved; we have to take it on trust and to hold it as a matter of faith.

Beyond all question, it may be a signal advantage to the actor that he can leave behind him nothing whereby his contemporary fame may be contested by those who come after him. How great an advantage it may be, we may gage by considering the sadly shrunken reputations to-day of certain speakers accepted in their own time as orators of compelling force. In the eighteenth century, Whitefield was a widely popular preacher, credited with genuine eloquence by all who heard him. One discourse of his was so moving that it coaxed the copper and the silver and the gold out of the pockets of the calm and unemotional Franklin. If we had only the testimony of those who heard him gladly, we could hardly fail to regard Whitefield as one of the really great orators of the world. Unfortunately for the fame of the fervid preacher, some of his sermons survive to bear witness against him. Whitefield's burning words, powerfully effective as they were when sustained by his artful delivery, are cold enough now that we have them on the printed page.

What happened to Whitefield in the eighteenth century is not unlike what happened to Gladstone in the nineteenth. There would be little possibility of denying to the great party-leader a foremost place among the world's mightiest orators, if we had only the record of the overwhelming effect produced upon those whom he addressed, whether he was carrying the fiery cross through Midlothian or holding the house entranced hour after hour by a speech on the budget. Not Webster, not Cicero, not Demosthenes was more powerful in producing results. But we are not compelled to rely solely on the recollections of those who sat silent under the spell of his commanding personality. When we seek to test Gladstone's title to be held a great orator, we can call other witnesses,—these very speeches themselves, revised by the speaker himself; and they bear testimony against him, just as Whitefield's sermons bear testimony against Whitefield.

The reputation of Gladstone and of White-field as orators would be higher than it is, if they were judged only by the memories of those who heard them, or by the record made by those who were still under the spell of their influence. Herein the actors are luckier than the orators, since it is by the enthusiastic record alone that they can be judged. There can be no other proof of their great gifts; and "none can test it."

XIII

IT is true that now and again a skeptic stands up to suggest a doubt whether the renowned actors of the past really deserved their reputations. He wonders how they would be received to-day, and whether we should esteem Burbage and Betterton and Edmund Kean as highly as they were once esteemed, each in his own day. He even ventures to opine that if these great actors could appear on our stage to-day, we should find them old-fashioned, of course, and probably also stilted and stagy. And altho this suggestion is disconcerting, it contains a certain measure of truth. The acting of the past was not exactly like the acting of the present, because the circumstances of performance have been continually changing, even if the principles of the art abide unaltered.

The actor must ever adjust himself to the theater in which he is performing. His methods must be modified in accordance with the condition of the stage at the time. Burbage played his parts on a bare platform thrust out into the unroofed yard; and Edmund Kean won his triumphs in a huge theater with the oil-footlights curving out far beyond the curtain. Burbage and Kean had to accept these conditions and to adjust their technic accordingly. If they were to appear to-day in the modern playhouse with its picture-frame stage, and if they were to act as they were wont to act in the wholly different playhouse of the platform-stage type, no doubt they would disappoint us, and we might easily fail to perceive their real merits. But this is not the fair way to put it. If Garrick were to be born again, and to grow up amid our conditions, he would accept these and find his profit in them. His histrionic genius would expand as freely now as it did then; and he would be as responsive to the pressure of public expectation in the twentieth century as he was in the eighteenth.

XIV

THERE are certain parrot-cries that are forever echoing down the corridor of Time. Every young generation hears·them, and is forced to wonder how much truth they may contain. Perhaps the most insistent of these immortal complaints is that which keeps on declaring the decline of the drama. That the theater is going to the dogs,—this is what we may hear on every hand. But a little knowledge of the last century is reassuring, since we learn then that our fathers and our grandfathers, and the grandfathers of our grandfathers, were all of them told that the stage had fallen on evil days and that its future would certainly be inferior to its past. Sometimes it is the organization of the theater which is said to be at fault; sometimes it is dearth of good actors; and sometimes it is the scarcity of good plays and the steady deterioration of the art of the dramatist.

When Colley Cibber asked Congreve why he did not write another comedy, the old wit retorted promptly, "But where are your actors?" And Colley Cibber was one of a group of actors and actresses as brilliant and as accomplished as ever graced the stage in Great Britain. Sir Philip Sidney almost wept over the pitiful con-

dition of the English drama, just before Shakspere came forward with his swift succession of
masterpieces. If we go back many centuries to
Greece, we find Aristophanes lamenting the
decay of dramatic literature as evidenced in
the plays of Euripides. And when Thespis first
started out with his cart,—the earliest recorded
attempt of any star-actor to go on the road with
his own company,—we may be certain that there
were not lacking veteran playgoers who promptly
foresaw the speedy decline of the drama.

Just now, at the beginning of the twentieth
century, when our theaters are more beautiful
and more artistically adorned than ever before,
and when scenery and costumes and all needful
accessories are more carefully considered, attention is loudly called to the feebleness of the
average play and to the inefficiency of the average actor. And yet a moment's reflection ought
to make it plain that there never has been any
period when the average play and the average
actor deserved unfailing praise. Even in the
greatest epochs of the drama the average play
was none too good. We are all familiar with
the comedies of Sheridan and Goldsmith; but
we do not recall the forgotten efforts of Cum-
berland and Kelly, who shared the stage with
them. We point with pride to Shakspere; but
we do not pine for a revival of the pieces of

Dekker and Heywood. We know that Corneille and Molière and Racine were the masters of the French theater under Louis XIV; but most of us are absolutely ignorant even of the faded names of their contemporary rivals.

Obviously it is unfair to crush the average playmaker of to-day by a comparison with the greatest dramatists of other days. And every one who has studied the recent history of the theater will admit, if he is both competent and candid, that the outlook for the future is far more hopeful than it was forty or fifty years ago. The technic of the dramaturgic art is far better understood now than it was a little while ago; and in every modern language there are men of ability who have mastered this technic and who are striving to set on the stage the themes, the manners, and the characters of this new century. Ibsen and Björnson are dead; but Hervieu and Brieux, Rostand and Lavedan, are writing in France, as Sudermann and Hauptmann are in Germany and d'Annunzio in Italy. In England there are Sir James Barrie and Mr. Shaw, Mr. Jones and Sir Arthur Pinero; and here in America there are half-a-dozen men, still young most of them, and still learning how to see the life about them and how to reproduce it on the stage, who are earnestly seeking as best they can to hold the mirror up to nature.

If the theaters are beyond all dispute better than they were a few years ago, and if the dramatic literature of the present bids fair to be more satisfactory in the future, the sole remaining point of attack is the acting. What is the profit in a rebirth of dramatic literature if there are no performers to embody it? Where are your actors? Where are the Booths, the Kembles, the Garricks of our time? Where is even that much-vaunted old-fashioned stock company, capable of presenting the old comedies because every member was a trained artist? With our syndicates and our star-system, and our long runs, the art of acting is doomed without hope of recovery. Who shall be bold enough to controvert prophecies of evil?

It calls for little hardihood to deny this and for little knowledge of the theater to disprove it. The Booths and the Kembles and the Garricks did not all live at once; and it is absurd to suppose that we can match all the mighty actors of the past in a single quarter of a century. We may even admit that the English-speaking stage happens for the moment to be without any histrionic artists of the acknowledged eminence of Irving and Jefferson and Booth. But to say this is not to admit that we are poverty-stricken, and that our theater is devoid of many players of admirable accomplishment both in Great Britain and the United States. We all know better. We can easily call the roll of a dozen or a score of actors who are artists, gifted by nature and cultivated by long exercise of their powers, possessing each of them an individuality of his own. Indeed, the list of these performers of high merit is so long that it would be invidious to attempt to set it down here. We can each of us make it up to suit our own likings.

XV

AND yet in fairness the admission must be made, not only that our stage just now happens to lack any performers of the acknowledged preëminence of Booth and Irving and Jefferson, but also that there is a fair foundation for the assertion that we do not now see the Old Comedies as well acted as they were a few years ago at Daly's, a little earlier at Wallack's, and still further back at the Haymarket in London. This admission can be made frankly and without also admitting that it implies any necessary degeneracy of the art of acting. The so-called Old Comedies—the 'School for Scandal,' the 'Rivals,' and 'She Stoops to Conquer'— were written for a theater in which the conditions were very different from those which obtain in

248

the playhouses of this twentieth century, and they called for acting different in kind from the acting appropriate on our modern stage.

Sheridan and Goldsmith wrote for a theater which was so insufficiently lighted that the stage had to curve far out into the auditorium, to form what was known as the "apron"; and on this apron, in the full glare of the footlights, the actor came forward, far in front of the proscenium-arch in which the curtain rose and fell. In our modern playhouses, every part of the stage is adequately illuminated by the electric light, and the apron has disappeared, so that the actor now does his work behind the proscenium-arch and remote from the audience. Half-a-century ago the actor was really performing on a platform thrust out into the audience, whereas to-day he is removed behind a picture-frame. The Old Comedies were written for the platform-stage, and they had the oratorical manner proper enough on a platform. Our modern plays are written for the picture-frame stage, and their dialog is far less rhetorical, far simpler, far more "natural" than was appropriate to the theater of the last generation.

It is no wonder, therefore, that the actors of our time, accustomed to these more natural modern pieces, have not preserved the artificial tradition established long ago for the proper performance of plays written to suit the very different conditions of an earlier theater that has now ceased to be. The best acting to-day is adjusted to the stage of to-day; and the best actors are striving for veracity of character-delineation of a kind almost impossible on the stage of yesterday. Their methods are necessarily different from the methods of their predecessors in the playhouses of half-a-century ago; but even if different, these methods are not necessarily artistically inferior. Ristori, for example, was reckoned a fine actress in her time, yet she would seem strangely old-fashioned, and perhaps even stagy, to us who were familiar with the simpler and profounder art of Duse. Ristori was a mistress of all the histrionic devices which belonged to the platform-stage, whereas Duse had adjusted her art to the later conditions of the picture-frame theater.

Probably very few of those who are studying the stage have yet seized the full significance of this change in the relation of the actor to the audience,—this withdrawal of the performer from the platform almost surrounded by the spectators behind a frame which sets him apart and keeps him remote. This modification of the circumstances of performance, like all other modifications that have preceded it in the long evolution of the theater, has had its effect on the dramatist as well as on the comedian. Duse was not more different from Ristori than is the 'Cavalleria Rusticana,' in which she appeared, different in its method from the 'Marie Antoinette,' in which the earlier Italian actress was so successful half-a-century ago. Of course, this change in the aims of the playwrights is not to be ascribed solely to the modification of theatrical conditions, for it is coincident also with the spread of realism. If Ibsen strove to present human nature as he saw it, with the utmost simplicity and directness, and if he eschewed rhetorical amplifications acceptable enough to our grandfathers, there is a double explanation. His attitude is partly the result of that wide-spread movement in favor of a bolder veracity than literature had aimed at before Balzac set the example; and it is also partly the result of the new opportunity proffered by the picture-frame of the modern theater, which seems to demand a more accurate reproduction of the characteristic background and a closer relation of character to environment.

There is no need of insisting that the more modern methods of the drama are better than the older. Indeed, the more we consider the conditions of the Greek theater and of the Elizabethan theater, the more clearly can we perceive that they also had advantages of their own not

to be found in the theater of our time. But it
is for the theater of our time that our dramatists must compose their plays; and it is in the
theater of our time that our actors must act.
The theater of the Greeks cannot be resusci-
tated to-day any more than the theater of the
Elizabethans. And it is with the theater of to-
day, and not with the theater of any yesterday,
that both playwright and performer have to
deal. Those who have the pleasant privilege
of advancing years, and who can therefore look
back to earlier conditions, may not like the
conditions that obtain now. And there is no
cause for wonder in the fact that some of them
think that the change is for the worse.

XVI

It will surprise no one to learn that Joseph
Jefferson found it difficult to reconcile himself
to the newer practices. He was himself an actor
who sought truth as he saw it; but he did not
relish the larger proportion of actual fact that
he found presented in certain recent plays. I
can recall a conversation with him during Duse's
first visit to the United States, not long after
he had seen her performance in 'Cavalleria Rusticana.' "It's too realistic," he said to me;

"altogether too realistic. Why, I could count all the fleas in that Italian village!"

And here is the difficulty of the modern school of actors. They are seeking to present character as sincerely as they can; they have relinquished many of the effects which actors of an earlier generation delighted in; and as a result they may sometimes seem tame and pale to those who are looking for the kind of acting which was appropriate enough in plays of a more florid type. It is this which underlay the complaint of the old actor in Sir Arthur Pinero's delightful 'Trelawney of the Wells,'—that the part given to him in the new play hadn't a single speech in it,—not what you could call a speech,—not a speech that you could "sink your teeth in"!

We need not be astonished that actors who overact their underacting should seem out of place and ill at ease in the older plays which abound in speeches that you can sink your teeth in. This is the chief reason why many recent revivals of old plays have seemed to us unsatisfactory. The actor was called upon to attempt something for which he had no training. He tried to apply modern methods to pieces which demanded insistently the fashions of an earlier time, and which lost much of their effect when they were not played in the key in which they were composed originally. To transpose them was to rob them of their special quality. And no better illustration of this could be found than the comparison of 'Fédora' as performed by Sarah-Bernhardt and by Duse. 'Fédora' is a show-piece, written around Sarah-Bernhardt; it is a play full of sound and fury, signifying nothing. Her performance of the part was incomparably brilliant, a masterpiece of bravura. The Italian actress, on the other hand, tried to make the character real and poignant; and this was patently impossible. The more veracious Duse was, the more she exposed the unveracity of Sardou. But a comparison of Duse and of Sarah-Bernhardt in a more modern play—in Sudermann's 'Heimat,' for example, which we know as 'Magda'—was altogether to the advantage of the younger performer.

XVII

"THERE are gains for all our losses," as the poet says,—even if there are also losses for all our gains. We lost something, no doubt, when the old stock companies passed out of existence, —such stock companies as the London Haymarket, or Wallack's, or Daly's. These companies contained many admirable actors who were accustomed to each other, and who understood all the advantages of team-play. But the actors of these companies played each of them his own "line of business," as it was called; and he was likely to play all his parts in much the same way. He did not realize that all acting ought to be character-acting. He was tempted to do his work in rough-and-ready fashion; and to repeat himself in every play in which he was called upon to appear.

Mr. George Bernard Shaw is a little overemphatic in expressing his contempt for the laziness and the incompetence only too often seen even in fairly good companies under the old conditions. "Having been brought up on the old stock-company actor," Mr. Shaw declares, "I knew that he was the least versatile of beings,—that he was nailed helplessly to his own line of heavy or light, young or old, and played all the parts that fell to him as the representative of that line in exactly the same way. I knew that his power of hastily swallowing the words of a part and disgorging them at short notice, more or less inaccurately and quite unimprovably (three months' rehearsal would have left him more at sea than three hours'), was incompatible with his ever knowing his part in any serious sense at all."

The answer to those who assert, truthfully enough, that the older plays are not now acted as well as they used to be, is that the newer plays are acted far better than they would have been in the days of the old stock companies. Performances like those of 'Secret Service,' of 'Arizona,' of 'Shore Acres,' of the 'Thunder-bolt,' were quite impossible under the earlier conditions. No doubt, there are failures enough to-day; but they are far fewer in our best theaters now than they were in the foremost playhouses of half-a-century ago.

I for one do not believe that the actors of our time are in any way inferior to the actors of the past, even if they do their work under different conditions. They may not succeed always when they attempt the plays of an earlier day, but their failure is not as complete as the failure of the older actors would be if it were possible to call upon them to appear in our modern realistic drama, where every part is more or less of a character-part, and where the actor, standing on a fully lighted stage, is expected to get his effect sometimes by his speech, but also often merely by a gesture or only by a look. Our actors are now less rhetorical and more pictorial,—as they must be on the picture-frame stage of our modern theater.

(1913)